FIRESIDE TALES

as Told by
Florida Cracker Cowboys

HOWARD S JONES JR

OTHER BOOKS BY THE AUTHOR

The Green Jeep—Recollections of a Boy and His Step-father in Florida Cracker Country, published in 2009, is a story of reclamation, set in the 1960's cow country in Okeechobee, Florida. It is a heart-warming and often hilarious tale of an immature boy becoming a man under the unconditional love and wisdom of a unique pioneer step-father and just a few of the Cracker characters at the ranch.

Other works in preparation include, A Glossary of Cracker Terms and Phrases—A Wealth of Barely Essential Information, where the author explains the commonly used Cracker terms and their humorous meanings and the contexts of use. All Creatures Mean and Tough, a working title, is a soon-to-be published. It is an account of the people, places, and things that a veterinary practitioner encounters in the Cracker cattle country of Florida. It includes wrecks, close calls, painful experiences, entertaining experiences and successes of his years in veterinary practice.

ACKNOWLEDGEMENTS

My thanks to the Crackers of Florida, including Partner Sills, Hubert Waldron, Junior Mills, Finis Harn, Solon Wilson, Gary Larsen, Steve, Ralph, and Fred Hartt, Bill Murphy, Wessel Durrance, Gator Taylor, Martin and Clarence Parnell, Wayne Collier, Rudy and Baby Ashton, Ephraim and Alfred Norman, Dennis McClelland, Dusty Young, Jack and Steve Skipper, Russell Lowe and, especially, Dr. Frank Handley

And to all who work on the ranches in the heart of Florida cattle country, and many others too numerous to mention.

To Hunter, my wife, for her tireless help in editing and encouraging; to Carlton Ward, Jr, for the cover photograph; and my close friend, Embellishment, for everything else.

TABLE OF CONTENTS

PREFACE

Each of these stories is written in a "stand-alone" arrangement and, therefore, has some repetition of facts and historical concepts. A few are versions of some classics *(Little Red Riding Hood, Chicken Little, Goldie Locks and the Three Bears, Jack and the Bean Stalk,* etc.) Others are pure fantasy, though some of the names used are from the historical records of the pioneer families in Okeechobee, Highlands, Glades and Hardee Counties. The majority are based on true tales *(Mama and the Doctor, The North Carolina Dogs, The Mexican Bulls, Poncho's Café, Loyalty, The Little Horse and the Boy,* etc.). For example, in *The North Carolina Dogs,* I vaccinated the dogs and the phrase, "Oh, by the way... I was the boy" in *The Little Horse and the Boy,* is a true statement. Hopefully, you will enjoy reading these tales as much as I have enjoyed writing them.

INTRODUCTION

I remember all the old tales that stirred my imagination. They were fun. But as I've grown older, I see a chance to spice them up a bit–in a way I've never seen before—in Cracker terminology. Now true Florida Crackers are frontiersmen or those with a pioneer mentality. The term is not necessarily pejorative for poor white Southerner. You find the frontier mentality in the West and the Southeastern region of America. Many Australians have a Cracker flavor to them. It's a mentality, a worldview—albeit a somewhat limited one at times—and a wonderful enjoyment of life and hard times. They think differently, act differently, work hard and enjoy life. They are a breed apart from the ordinary and are dying out as modern culture takes dominance. I was fortunate in living for many years in that culture in the cow country of Florida where there resides to this day little clusters of Cracker families. Oh, the young ones are driving jacked-up trucks and all, but they are not far from their grandparents in the pioneer mentality.

Golf courses now take some of the land where cattle once roamed. Shopping centers cover the abandoned gopher tortoise's holes. Florida Jays and Bob White quail have moved to the woods near subdivisions. Dozens of dilapidated cow pens dot the landscape where raw-boned sweaty cowboys worked their free-roaming cattle in muddy pens, in heat, flies, mosquitoes and lightening strikes like you've never seen. It has all changed just in the last forty-five years. I love the flavor of the old Florida, the humor and the uniqueness of the true Florida Crackers. I met some of similar types of pioneer people in Colorado, Texas, Oklahoma, Arizona, New Mexico, Georgia, Alabama, Mississippi, Louisiana, and even in Western North Carolina, Kentucky and Tennessee. They were separate from the Florida Cracker but many had the same twinkling eye.

So today, we have a chance to rewrite the old tales, the classics that enthralled generations and some that are not so classical. Now the cracker terms and phrases may be unusual to most. I don't expect this will be funny to young children but it may be a side-splitter for the older ones (and their parents) that know the classic tales by heart. The idea developed over many years when my family used to play a story-telling game called, "You Take It!"

The game started with a theme story. The first teller would start a story in basic form. Coming to a key point in the story, he or she would turn to another one, saying, "You Take It!" The chosen one would then begin his or her imaginative version of the story. Of course, they added their own embellishments. Off we would go in an entirely different direction. Some tales that started with a boy lost in the woods would end up on a space ship or in a version of a Louis L'Amour book. You never knew where it would end. (The only thing that worked better at putting the children to sleep was lectures on Enteric Diseases of Neonatal Dairy Calves.) Nevertheless, it worked wonders for the minds of the children. Their imaginations grew and grew. I must admit that I enjoyed the mental acrobatics of "taking it" after a little girl had gotten frozen in a water bucket while a wolf was sharpening his skinning knife. It made no sense at times but the children just hooted in laughter—the crazier the circumstances, the funnier the story became.

I have searched for a proper name for this pitiful work. I thought of, *A Cracker Veterinarian's Versions of the Classics*, or, *Son! Now that's the way it ought to be told!* But in the end, I decided to tell it like I'm telling it to my grandchildren, as *Fireside Tales as Told by Florida Cracker Cowboys.*

CHAPTER ONE

LITTLE RIDING RED

The Story of a Little
Cracker Gal in Ol' Time Florida

I remember a time when there was a little gal named Red Hood. The Hoods were originally from Pahokee. She and her family lived not far from Fisheatin' Creek, on the west side of the Big Lake. One day her mama ast her to take a poke of guavas, a pound of grits and some fatback to her granny. Red and Granny weren't much good in the cow pens—Red was too little and Granny was too old and feeble. Granny had sent word that she was feelin' poorly, so Mama ast Red to go and cheer her some.

So Paw helps Red saddle her little pony mare, named Lightnin'. Red pulls out about first light with the poke tied to the saddle horn. Lots of people think the woods is a terrible place to go but it is a lot safer than town on Sad'day night.

1

Anyways, as she was riding among the palmettos, a panther pops up. Now this weren't no ordinary panther—he was wearing some bib overalls with a red bandana aroun' his neck. (Some say that he got them off'n a fella that was clearin' five acres near Palmdale.)

The panther sez, "Whut you packin' in that poke?"

She sez, "Ah'm takin' sum fat-back, grits and guavas to my granny."

"Ya know, it ain't real safe for a little girl to be alone in the woods," the panther said.

Red said, "Hit don't make me no nevermind since I am carryin' this here .22 pistol in my saddle bags. Now if'n you will git out the way, I got bidness to attend to."

Red clucked to Lightnin' and off they went toward the creek.

Now the panther knew a quicker route—he cut across the swamp and came out at Granny's cabin. He bust down the door, ate Granny—flour-sack print dress and all. This weren't no easy feat since he was already full of Palmdale farmer. He changed from the overalls to Granny's bed robe that hung on a nail near the bed. He stuffed the overalls under Granny's bed and then crawled under her bed chivers.

Red rides up a little later, ties her pony to a myrtle bush, and goes in tha house. She said, "Hello the house! Granny, hits me. I brung some fresh-picked guavas and some grits and fat back for you."

From the bed, the panther sez, "Well, don't this beat all—I wuz jus thinkin bout you all... Come closer girl, my glasses ain't working too good this mornin'."

Red sez, "Oh, I forgot you couldn't see me from this far—SON! Yer eyes sure are big this morning!"

"They helps me see you better," replied the panther.

Now Red weren't no mean child and was careful not to hurt her elder's feelin's, but she noticed the big nose of the panther.

She sez, "Dang, Granny! I don't remember yer nose bein' so big and black!"

The panther replied, "Oh, I bin readin' the Bible and you know how close I git to the pages."

Then Red gits a reel close look at the fangs of the panther and sez, "Granny, what huge teeth you have!"

The panther leaps at her and grabs her by his claws and smacks his lips, ready to eat her.

Ol' Red gets all skeered and screams out—after all she weren't nuthin but a little girl—and she didn't have a lighterd knot or carry a pocketknife or nuthin'!

Her scream carried a piece into the woods and wuz heard by a man coming by to drop off a pig for Granny. He pulls his rifle out the scabbard, dropping the pig in the pen, he runs in with a serious intent to do harm to anyone who would hurt a child. He bust in the door and finds Red in the clutches of a panther dressed up like a woman. He lifts his gun up, centers the barrel between the panther's eyes. It wuz like a covey of quails coming out a gopher hole. The panther drops Red and bounds for the window. The Cracker man fires at the panther—missing him and hitting a skillet hung on the wall. The bullet ricochets

3

off the skillet and hits Granny's spurs, then it thuds harmless in the Farmer's Almanac on the table.

The panther makes it to the yard but all the excitement and activity, with him being full of farmer and all, he stops in the yards and coughs up Granny like a yard cat does a wad of hair. Granny is not worse for the wear but she wuz a mite peeved about the whole ordeal. She said, "I be John Brown if I didn't git caught flat-footed with that panther…" Her flour sack print dress wuz all wrinkled and wet and she held what looked like the tongue of a brogan boot in her hand—from the Palmdale farmer, I suspect.

Bless his heart, the Cracker man saved the day, but I don't see how the panther coulda ate Red–after eatin' the farmer <u>and</u> Granny! Anyways, they all put on a pot of coffee and started cookin' the grits. The panther escaped to the woods. He figured he'd come back later when things settled down for the new pig. Granny went to the creek to warsh off while Red chunked pine cones and lighterd knots at the little gators that came to inspect the goin's on.

So they had a fine meal of grits, fried fat back, swamp cabbage, gravy, biscuits and guava cobbler. Then they sat on the front porch, talkin' about the woods and the weather. Red rode back home after dark with her .22 pistol in her hand. Mama ast her, "Well, girl? How's Granny?"

Red replied, "She's fine, Mama. We had a tussle with a panther but we worked it all out."

CHAPTER TWO

GOLDI LOCKS AND THE THREE HOGGS

*I've heard it said that one should
never try to teach a hog to sing—
It's a waste of time and irritates the hog.
–An Old Kentucky Proverb*

Deep, deep in the piney flatwoods, across Boggy
Branch, near the big palmetto patch, lived a family of
hogs—Pappy Hogg, Mama Hogg and Baby Hogg—
and they lived there close to the oak hammock near
Opal. Most of the Hogg family had split up for various reasons. Some of the local hog hunters came
through about a week before and nearly cleaned out
the whole bunch, leaving only these three to carry
on the family name. The Hogg family was a proud
bunch. They'd lived near Opal for generations, rip-
ping up pastures for grubs and such. Times were generally purty good for them but lately it had been a bit
tite. The acorn crop was poor this year and the turkeys had beat them to the best part of them. Anyways,

they tried to make it in spite of the poor pickin's. Somehow a steady diet of grubs and frogs ain't real satisfyin'.

One day, in the middle of the day's foraging, they happened upon a hunter's camp. They were delighted to find a Dutch Oven in the coals of an oak fire. Papa Hogg rummaged around and found three spoons and tin pie-pans. He tipped the lid off the Dutch Oven, dipping generous servings of chicken pilau, which we call "perlue", for all the Hoggs to enjoy. The dang stuff was blistering hot, so they sat the pans aside to let them cool. Mama Hogg heard a raccoon squall nearby, so they decided to go see what the fuss was all about whilst the perlue cooled a mite.

Once they were out of sight, up rides Goldi Locks Mac Gruder, a local cowgirl and hunter. She was starved half to death. She'd been out cow huntin' all morning and was ready for a hot dinner. Goldi was a Celtic lass—blonde haired and blue eyed. She was not bad to look at—especially after she had warshed her face. She set about eatin' her dinner when up walks the Hogg family. Papa Hogg, being the biggest and meanest of the bunch, walked slightly ahead of the others. He stopped and sniffed the air. He said, "I think we best be careful—I smell a human in the camp."

"Ah thank," said Mama Hogg. Baby Hogg walked a little to the side of his papa and smelled the air. Sure enough they winded the smell of perfume and sweaty leather.

Baby said, "Hut chall wanna do?"

"We best go see whut she's up to—this makes me a little tight-jawed," said Papa.

Goldi was working on the second pan when they walked into camp.

Papa Hogg said, "Whut in the ham fat are you doin', gal? Don't you know we dipped up that perlue for ourselves?"

"Oh," cried Goldi, "I didn't know y'all wuz comin back."

"Yeah, you best take notice of such things before you come into someone's camp and eat their groceries," grumbled Papa Hogg.

Goldi said, "Well, Mr. Smarty-breeches, whose camp is this anyways?"

"I reckon you got us there," replied Mama Hogg.

They all dipped up helpin's of perlue and set to eatin'. Goldi eyed them between spoonfuls and finally said, "What y'all gonna do tonite?"

"Oh, we figured we'd ease on down to the marsh and see if they put some cow feed in the feeders," said Papa Hogg.

Goldi thought a moment and then said, "Look, it don't sound like y'all have a whole lot goin' on—why don't y'all go to town with me?"

"I declare," said Mama. "What in the world would we do in town?"

Goldi grinned and said, "Ther's gonna be a buck-out at the Speckled Perch Café—I'd love to see y'all run through all them folks in the bar."

The whole Hogg family laughed at the prospect of runnin' helter-skelter through all the people in the middle of a dance. "We've always wanted to do some meanness in town. Could we really go with you?" said Papa.

"Sure," said Goldi. "I'll go git my truck and y'all can ride in the back."

So she finished her second plate of perlue, tightened up her saddle cinch while the Hoggs ate their meals, and rode off in the night. She came back in about half an hour. Her truck had big wheels and was jacked up so high that she had to back down in a ditch so the Hoggs could load up in the back. They laughed and joked around about the fun that was about to occur. Goldi put a tarp over them. Papa said, "Now let's us all lay real quiet so's we don't rurn the surprise." So the Hogg family settled down for the ride to town.

Through the town they went, running the stoplights and signs. Goldi pulled up to the back of the Speckled Perch Café. The parking lot was full of trucks, cars, and trailers containing quiet horses standing on three legs. Goldi slipped over to the back door and opened it about a foot wide. The Hogg family darted out the truck and ran full bore, no pun intended, through the kitchen into the dining area to the dance floor. They started squealing and ran through startled dancers, under the tables of people who were having a beverage of some kind.

Baby Hogg ran up under a girl who was dressed in tight jeans and white cowgirl shirt. She screamed at the sight of him and crawled on a table. A fight broke out as everyone figured it was one of the men who scared tha' gal. The Hoggs screamed so loud it'd make you deaf. They'd stop for an instant and look for packs of people gathered together—then they'd run right under them, scatterin' everyone this way and that. Goldi laughed so hard her sides hurt.

It wuz plum pandemonium when it broke forth. Bottles flew, fists swung, glass broke and people were screaming for help like little girls. The bar tender pulled his shot-gun but couldn't get a clear shot since the Hoggs kept moving amide all the legs. The band kept playing like nuthin' out the ordinary was happening. Fact it, some folks jus' kep dancin'! Finally, Goldi whistled real loud and the Hoggs darted for the door. She let the tailgate down and they loaded up. Three cur dog puppies joined them in the back of the truck. They drove back to the ranch, laughing and replaying the scene to the delight of the pups.

They stopped at a hammock and built a fire. Goldi made coffee. She poured them all a cup in pans, cups and bowls she kept in the truck. They laughed and talked a lot—about the stars, the night sounds and the "ritchets" and "wheears" of the frogs.

Papa Hogg said, "I 'spect that was the bes' time I ever had. Y'all up for it next Sat'day nite?"

"Ah thank!" said Baby.

"Yeah', they all agreed.

Goldi Locks said, "Meet y'all here bout dark next Sad'day."

So for many, many times they made the trip to the Speckled Perch. The folks there got to lookin' for them. It got to be a show of sorts. But they had to change their ways a bit. It got sos people wuz waitin' outside for the show each Sad'day night. The owner of the bar complained some but soon saw this wuz a good deal for him. Goldi wore different wigs and even dressed up like a preacher's wife, a IRS tax auditor and even a county health inspector—that fooled a lot of them. She borrowed different trucks, trailers and cars to try to fool the people. The Hoggs tried different hats and caps, and shirts with numbers from 1 to 23 with two shirts numbered with 12 on them. They'd run outside, change caps and shirts and reappear. This confused many people—they thought there were many more Hoggs than was actually there. 'Course, some of them wuz slightly snockered on strong beverages and such. They even used various colors of paint on their bodies, to try to add a little variety. Papa Hogg once did his impression of a Peacock but nobody laughed.

The last I heard, Baby wuz livin' there—dancin' with the gals, servin' drinks, makin' deviled eggs, loadin' supplies; and he sang some, though he wadn't good at playin' the steel geetar, 'cause he didn't have any thumbs! His mama and daddy wuz real proud that he was makin' a way for hisself in the world. They laughed when Goldi told them that she was

10

also proud of Baby, saying, "That goes to show you that even a blind hog will find an acorn ever now and then." (She meant he was real lucky. Yeah, she knew it was a play on words... course Baby weren't blind, but he wuz a Hogg.)

So if y'all want to see a sight, go down and hang out at the Speckled Perch Café on Sad'day night. Baby might even fix you a cool drink or sing for ya. The rest'll be along sometime later.

CHAPTER THREE

WO SNITE AND THE DEVILIN' SWARFS

Oncst upon a time there was a wicked woman. She was meaner than a snake. She lived with a hen-pecked man at the Ol' Evans Place. She ruled a family with her meanness. All the nearby neighbors were plum intimidated by her venom. There was an orphaned girl there named Wo Snite. Where she came from and who her family wuz, no one knew. She just showed up one day on the doorstep of the queen of the community. The ol' wicked woman took Wo in and made her work for her keep. Wo warshed dishes, cooked fatback, worked the garden, ironed cloths and swept the cabin out every day. She tried to stay out the way of the mean woman. The woman had a mirror that she adored herself in. One day she asked the mirror:

> "Mirror, Mirror on the table,
> Am I as fair as Betty Grable?"

The mirror replied:

"I see you standing there with hands on hips; I know
my answer will chap your lips.
No doubt my answer will cause a fight,
But there ain't none purtier than Little Wo Snite."

This really did chap the lips of this queen of the settlement. She told her hen-pecked husband to take Wo Snite out and kill her in the woods. But he reneged, letting Wo Snite go. She pulled out for the deep woods, finally coming to a cabin. It was a bit worse for the wear. There were pigs in a pen, a horse stable, and an orphaned calf in one of the horse stalls. She knocked on the door but there wuz no answer. She ate a couple of guavas off the tree next to the porch. Then she crawled into a hammock that was strung out between two porch posts and took a nap.

Just before dark, the seven Swarf brothers rode in from a hard day of cow huntin'. They unsaddled at the little barn and walked to the cabin. As I said there were seven of them: Finis, Ephraim, Hubert, Boy, Ralph, Gator and Minnerhead. The boy's parents were dead—they died in a cabin fire one cold night many years ago. The boys had mite near raised themselves. They were a hard-working lot but a little on the rank side. People all around knew the Swarfs as a rough crowd. That's how they came to be known as the "Devilin' Swarfs". They'd pull all kinds of tricks and pranks on neighbors. One time they put a skunk

14

in the outhouse at the little cabin school. Another time they dressed up a pig in a dress, turning it loose at a church picnic. They did wild things, too. One of them climbed a cabbage palm and wouldn't come down. His brothers cut the palm down with an axe while he fanned it with his hat, yelling, "I'm ridin' 'er down Boys!" How Minnerhead, the Odes (that is, the *oldest* son) got his name, no one knows.

"I wish you'd look," said Ephraim.

"Yeah, look what the hogs drug up," said Boy, "let's put her in the pig pen."

"Leave 'er alone—she ain't hurtin' nobody," growled Minnerhead.

Wo woke with a start and said, "Please don't hurt me—I didn't mean no harm. I escaped from the old woman at the Evans Place. I've walked all day."

The boys commenced to fight about it. It was butt over teakettle—elbows, fists, hats and boots flew as the tussled in the yard—a regler fist-city. Wo slipped off the porch and ran into the woods. She was all the way to Panther Ford when Minnerhead trailed her up.

"Why did you leave? There ain't nuthin' between here and Ft. Greene. Come stay with us. We need a girl's touch around the cabin. We're rougher than corncobs." he said.

Wo smiled and said, "Okay."

So the Devilin' Swarfs agreed to let her stay if she'd make the biscuits since Ralph didn't do such a good job of cookin' them. She agreed. They gave her a little room to herself and she grew to love the family of cantankerous boys. The first thing she did was to put up some frilly curtains. Every day Minnerhead would smile at her—she liked that.

Meanwhile, at the Evans Place, the queen-woman happened to see her mirror again. She asked:

> "Mirror, Mirror, on the bureau,
> Am I as purty as Greta Garbo?"

The mirror replied:

> "Now I ain't one to spread gossip or bad-talk, nor
> give much of a shout,
> But next to Wo, you look like an earthworm
> with his guts slung out."

Now this just hair-lipped the queen. She shouted, "But she's dead!"

The mirror said:

> "Now, now, don't git yer knickers in a twist.
> It'll do you no good at me to shake yer fist."

The ol' wicked woman was madder than a dirt dauber in a fruit jar. She pitched another fit and, as they say in these parts, "she showed her country behind." The neighbors said some of her screams were mite near eight foot long. She swore she'd

16

destroy that girl with gossip and slander. Her poor hen-pecked husband went on a long huntin' trip. He tossed his hat in the door when he got back to see if she'd rip it to shreds. She did. He went back to the woods.

A month later after she'd cooled off a little and had spread most of her venom, she asked the mirror:

> "Mirror, Mirror on the wall,
> Now who's the fairest of them all?"

The mirror said:

> I 'spect you're so mean
> That you'll always be the queen."

The mean ol' woman said,

> "Whut you talkin' bout,
> You silver-covered glass?"

The mirror replied:

> "Shoo-tee! I know this'll give you a fright.
> There still ain't none pertier'n Little Wo Snite."

The queen wuz madder'n ah baptized cat. She continued her slander and called on others to join her. After all she was the queen and ruler of the community. People just paid her no never mind.

Meanwhile, Minnerhead Swarf asked Wo Snite to marry him. She accepted his proposal. He was a good man. He wasn't purty, nor wuz he the sharpest axe in the barn, but he was a solid man and would be faithful to Wo. He worked cattle, did his own blacksmithing and saddle repairs. He gardened, cow hunted, hog hunted, fished, cut cabbages and taught his brothers and all his children how to live off the land. Minnerhead smiled at Wo every single day and she always smiled back. They had five sons and five daughters and by the last count they had 28 grand children. He sold cattle in Ft. Pierce and Tampa— always bringing the gold back to bury in the ground near their home. They had a chest full under their bed. They rarely needed gold since he was so good at caring for his family.

Years later, the wicked queen died. She was angry mean 'til her last breath. Some say it wuz the anger that finally got her. Her family gave the mirror to Wo Snite Swarf. The hen-pecked husband opened up a fruit stand on the edge of town. He sold the family farm for mite near a million dollars. He bought a ten-acre lot in the pines of Alabama and put a double wide trailer on it—like he'd always dreamed of doin'. One of his sons is a noted psychologist, practicing in New York City.

One day, many years later, Wo paused before the mirror. She blew a strand of hair out of her eyes, closely inspecting her face. She'd wrinkled some in

all the years with children, but she just couldn't resist
asking the mirror:

> "Mirror, Mirror on the wall,
> Who's the fairest of them all?"

The mirror shined anew and said:
"Oh, there's more beautiful, younger and smarter
than you,
But I declare there's none better.
For outer beauty, like a flower, fades away,
But godly children are a blessing for many a day.

So in this, Wo Snite Swarf, you exceed—
You've raised your family in goodness with care—
You're just the very best mother and the most fair."

CHAPTER FOUR

JACK AND THE BEAN SPROUT

*In Georgia, the legend says
that you must close your windows
at night to keep it out of the house.
The glass is tinged with green, even so...*
From the poem, "Kudzu,"
by James Dickey

Oncst upon a time, on a little homestead in South Florida, there lived a little boy named Jack. He lived with his mama. He was named after his father, who had died in a logging accident. Mama nicknamed him "Pooter", but she was the only one who called him that. It was a hard life there ever since they moved there from Kentucky. Things got tite for them. There just wadn't enough to go around with the cow and all. Mama told Jack that he would have to sell the cow to have enough money for essentials for the next winter. They would need some side bacon—sometimes she called it salt pork—and some coffee, grits and plenty of dried soup beans. The cow was a pitiful thing—she looked puny and wormy. You could count her ribs by shining a flashlight through her rib cage. They had fed her some Beechnut Chewing Tobacco for the worms but it didn't seem to help her gain weight. Jack speculated that it might be the fact that she had poor teeth. Anyways, Jack was a good boy—he always obeyed his mama.

He tied the cow's horns with a string to lead her and he saddled his horse, pulling out for the far country before first light. On the way to Yee Haw Junction, he met a man who was coming down the road. The man was walking with a cabbage palm fan in each hand. He was frantically swatting with "slap-slaps" at the mosquitoes that fogged in around his head and body. Jack said, "Them mosquitoes are rank, ain't they?" The man said, "Yeah, just wait 'til you git to Osceola County—ther' rough up there!" The man inquired where Jack was headed. He told him that he wuz gonna sell the cow for his mama. The man figured that he mite clear ten dollars, if he was lucky. Jack told him a goodbye and pulled out to the north.

It seemed to Jack that he had traveled for months, but it really was only about two hundred and fifty-eight days. His trail took him up the Kissimmee valley, meandering next to the river on cow trails and old wagon tracks. He went through some wild country. The travelin' was tough at time—there were no trails in places. He just kept goin' north. He noticed the land began to change from marshes to sand hills and sometimes, big prairies. He went through the old Indian campsites in Ocala and other places. A man he met on the trail told him that the Seminole used to go to Ocala for the summers and down to Okeechobee for the winters because of the mosquitoes. He had to admit that them things tormented him at times, too. Why he had to spend the night in a lake once because of them. His horse and the cow fidgeted all night that time, walkin' under cabbage fans to keep the things off'n their bodies. He went by Ft. Hogtown and ever northward, past marshes, piney flat woods, and hammocks.

He spent the night in barns, under oak trees, on sand banks near creeks, on open prairies and in cabbage hammocks. He even had to sleep in a tree oncst, over a big campfire because of a panther. All the while he lived off the land. The cow seemed content to walk along, grazing here and there. He met farmers, a few Yankee tourists, Seminoles, a surveyor, cattlemen, gator hunters, fishermen, gardeners, woodcutters, a train conductor and three preachers. None of them were interested in his cow—although the surveyor offered him a fruit jar of whisky for her.

Sometimes he'd take a day of two to go around what seemed like hundreds of lakes and deep creeks, rivers or swamps. He'd have to hunt to find river crossings. He even rode a ferry once. He saw all kinds of wildlife—deer, turkey, ducks, and snakes of all kinds. He saw quail, possum, panther, eagles, buzzards, egrets, and hundreds of water birds, fat brown bears, curious gators, coons and laughing otters, and even some wild cattle. All kinds of small varmints were around, too. The land changed from sandy to hard clay soils. He seemed to steadily get higher in elevation—it was gradual but higher nonetheless. The trees and grasses changed, too. The weather changed. The nights shortened and the days grew longer as he traveled. He'd started his trip in the early spring, when he could see his breath at times. It was now goin' on winter.

Finally one day he met a man who was driving wagon being pulled by a black mule. Jack asked him, "Jus zackly where am I?"

The man said, "Son, you're in Georgie."

"Well, I swan," said Jack, "I come a fer piece from Florida, ain't I?"

He asked the man if someone might be interested in buying a cow, who was fat by now from all the trail grazing. The man sent him to the local cow trader.

The cow trader was a little on the paunchy side of things but he seemed to be honest. Jack spoke to him about the buying of his cow. The man looked at her, circling around, chewing on a cigar as he did it. He finally said, "Boy, I'll give you three bean sprouts for this cow."

Jack wondered if this was a good deal. "Whut in the world will I do with bean sprouts? What are they good for?"

"Why," the man said, "Ther' good for the soil and grow real fast. They'll cover your farm in no time.

You can make flour out of the leaves and the critters can eat their fill."

Jack thought about how poorly the farm was and said he'd take the deal—he was tired of dragging that ol' cow anyways. The man went behind his barn and came out with a gunnysack that had the bottom filled with dirt and the green leaves of three little plants sticking out the open end. Jack handed over the cow lead and took the sack. He pulled out for home. He made good time on the way back since he was finally shut of the cow.

When he got home, he showed Mama his little plant called "bean sprouts." She was madder than he'd ever seen her. She grabbed the sack and threw it out the window. "Ca-lump!" went the sack when it hit the sand. Jack cried that night. The next morning Jack wiped the sleep from his eyes and noticed that a green tint was all around the windows. He went over to the window, poking his head through the leaves to look outside.

The whole house wuz covered by these plants! He took a kitchen knife and cut his way out to look around. The house was completely hidden behind a solid wall of broad green leaves.

He went in the house looking for Mama. All he found was a note pinned to the front curtain that said, "Boy, I can't take it anymore—I've gone to Miamah to see your aunt. Be a good boy. I know you can do alrite without me. Love, Mama." Well sir, Jack set to. He got a grubbing hoe, an axe and a butcher's knife and he took to cuttin' away the plants. He'd cut openings on one side of the house but by the time he got back around where he started, the dang things had growed over the windows again! All that day and the next week, he cut and cut and hacked at the bean sprouts. He never saw any beans. He swore that it seemed to grow a foot a day—it even growed while he took a nap. Dangest things he'd ever seen.

Then one day, as Jack made another run at cutting away the bean sprouts, he heard the thunder of hooves and the yips of a man, like when he is calling his dogs. He poked his head through the leaves at the window and saw the biggest man he'd ever seen. It was Big John, locally called "The Giant". He was indeed huge. He sat a big horse and must have weighed way over half the weight of a fat bull yearling. Big John was a sight to behold. He hollered, "Fee! Fie! Get behind! Foe, Go ahead! Fum! Side thisaway!" He cracked a long whip to get everyone's attention. "schur-Ka-TOW!" it sounded. He called the dogs, saying, "Hold'em, boys." The dogs ran in great circles, forcing the cattle to bunch up in a tite herd.

He drew his horse up, looking at the pile of green leaves with Jack's head sticking out a hole. "SON! Whut in the world are you doin' in a pile of leaves?"

Jack slipped out the window and walked over to Big John. "I been trimmin' these bean sprouts for nigh on ta ten days now—I cain't seem to get 'em beat back."

"It's no wonder," said Big John, "That's *Puerania montana*! It looks like the *lobata* variety. Yeah, it's kudzu alright!"

26

"Whut in the green earth is kudzu?" asked Jack.

"Why it's a plant from over in the orient sommers. It'll take the place if'n you don't kill it back!" said Big John.

Jack asked him then if he wanted a cup of coffee. Big John said that would be mighty fine. So Jack made a fire, drew up pond water in a pot and built the coffee. He and Big John sat under a little oak tree, drinkin' coffee and watchin' the kudzu grow. Finally Jack asked him, "Where'd you git them yearlings?"

Big John's voice boomed, "I jus' bought 'em. I'm looking for some pasture to fatten them up."

Jack thought about this and finally suggested, "You say this here kudzu is good to eat? Why don't you let them eat the leaves off'n the house? My neighbor has some goats that we could borrow and we have some chickens that could help out, too."

"Good idea," said Big John. So he called for Fee, Fie and the other two dogs and had them work the yearlings over around the house. While the yearlin's started eatin', Big John and the dogs went for the goats. They returned with the little herd of goats the next mornin' and the chickens seemed to enjoy rummaging around in the kudzu, too. They all set to eatin' it faster'n a duck on a June bug. Five weeks later parts of the house were visible again. Jack and John killed a deer and made some jerky. They ate fried fish, grits, tomato gravy and biscuits, guavas and fried venison for several days. In another week, they moved into the house.

During these times, Jack and Big John talked a lot. As the cattle and goats ate the kudzu, they became fast friends. Several months passed. The yearlings were fatter than town dogs by this time. They decided to go into bidness together. They formed the 2-J Ranch on Big John's property—just north of the nearby county line. They also opened a bar-be-que café on the edge of town. Their sign said, "Big John and Pooter's Bar-Be-Que—All free-ranging, Kudzu-fed Beef, Goat and Chicken." The café took off—especially after folks got a dose or two of Mama's recipe for Bucksnort Beans. It's said that the Ashley Gang ate there once. This was just before the law gunned them down on a bridge. People came from as far away as Tater Hill, Hole-in-the-wall and East Berea to eat their bar-be-que and beans. The ranch did reel good, too.

John went on to become a State Senator. When you take a close look at the county maps, you'll see a place where there is a jog in the county lines between two South Florida counties. The reason for this relocation of the line was to incorporate the 2-J Ranch into the southern county and allow Big John to run for the Senate. Both counties liked the idea. The one northern county was willin' to give up land so Big John would not take the seat of their Senator. The southern county that gained the Ranch property was pleased to have Big John as one of their Senators.

Jack became a prominent bidnessman. He bought a fishing shack at Chokoloskee and sent money to his mama in Miamah. It is said that she moved out on a beach somewhere near there and started a bingo parlor.

Every year the kudzu comes back. Big John and Jack run in about 500 heads of yearlings for fattening after it gits goin' reel good. Life is good for them now. A little over a year after the 2-J Ranch formed, the ol' cow that Jack had sold came back home. She brought a yearling and a newborn calf with her. She was fat and perty. Jack had the start of his own herd now. The 2-J Ranch really got big then. He named his three head, "A Hundred or So", "Couple A Hundred" and "A Few More." If anyone asked him how many head he had, he'd say, "A Hundred or So is on the north side of the house, Couple A Hundred is in the East pasture and A Few More is close to the house."

Fee, Fie and Foe retired from their cow huntin' bidness but Fum still works part time and does some consulting. Big John sits on his assets up in Tallahassee. Jack occasionally goes out to the old homestead place some—especially after a fine barbe-que beef and beans dinner. He'll draw up a pot of pond water and make coffee. He sits under the little oak, watching the turkeys and quails feeding, the armadillos rummaging around looking for grubs and the squirrels playing tag in the trees. Every now and again, he'll take out his cow whip and make it pop, "schur-Ka-TOW", to hear tha echo of the pow it makes again in the woods. He's a good man, tougher than a bus station steak.

CHAPTER FIVE

CHICKEN LITTLE

This here is my version of the story of Chicken Little. Oncst upon a time there was a young fella named Chick Little. His friends called him "Chicken". It had nothing to do with his being cowardly yellow or such as that, although he was a little afraid of chickens. In fact he was anything but a cowardly chicken. It had to do with family names. There had been several in the Little family named Chick. There wuz Chick Cletus Little, Chick Oban Little, Chick Ray Little, Patricia Chick Little, cousin Finis Chick O'Berry and Aunt Chickalina Mae Little Johnson. All of them except Chickalina were comfortable with their names. She was a bit touchus about her's, preferring Mae instead. They all learned to fight at an early age. They wuz raised in a backwoods area of South Florida, near Lake Okeechobee. But everyone knew that Chick was afraid of chickens but they also knew he would knock a knot on yer head if you teased him about it. He wuz afraid of little green tree frogs, too. (I heard it told that one jumped on his face while he wuz havin' a bad dream once—though nobody knows if that's all for sure.) He accepted the name Chicken, in light of the Chick name—not because he was afraid of chickens and green frogs.

One day, cow prices went to the bottom of the barrel. He had taken some butcher cows to the sale and only got about 10 cents a pound. By the time the market took out their sale fee, ther' weren't much left. Wellsir, ther's no way a fella can make it in the cattle bidness at that price. He come home all upset about it. He said, "The sky is fallin' in on me." He cranked the phone and called his friend down the road apiece, Skinny Penny Parnell. He told her, "The sky's fallin in—cow prices have hit the lowest in fifty years!" Skinny Penny said, "Yeah, tell me 'bout it. I never seen prices so low."

Skinny Penny Parnell wuz really skinny. They say she could stand under a cloths line and keep out the rain. It wuz rumored that she never got wet in the wood, since she could run from tree to tree and never get touched by raindrops. She said she did in fact do this and that she heard that is the same way that leprechauns got such a bad reputation. She paid no never mind to the name. Fact is she was meaner than a gator. She got used to it however and didn't knock any more teeth out after the eighth grade.

They decided to talk with Goosey Lucy Williams. Now Goosey was a fine gal, but she wuz a bit nervous. It all started in grade school when the boys would job her with sticks and with their thumbs. She'd be getting on the slide, they'd goose her from behind and she'd jus' go plum crazy. She'd squall out in a shrill scream and slap who ever wuz behind her. 'Course, this wuz great sport among the class boys. They named her Goosey Lucy and it stuck. She was always fidgety and nervous. When she got real excited, she'd cuss like a sailor and bark like a dog. But when you could git her attention, she wuz smart and knew some stuff about cattle. She too wuz concerned by the all time low in cow prices.

So Chicken Little, Skinny Penny and Goosey Lucy had a serious talk about the situation. "Girls, the sky's fallin' in on us. We'll go broke in a year if things don't improve" said Chicken as he chewed on a sliver of grass.

"Ah thank!" said Skinny Penny, as she spit on the sand.

"Tell me 'bout it," said Goosey Lucy, as she jumped as a fly went by her head.

"We need sum more money to operate," said Chicken, as he again spit on the sand.

"Right," said the girls in unison, as they both spit on the sand.

"Whut if we borrowed sum money from the banker, Lochy Foxx?" asked Skinny Penny.

"Mite work," said Goosey Lucy.

"How much do y'all think we ought to borrow?" said Skinny, "We ought to give it a try."

Goosey said, "I 'spect it'll take 'bout $60,000 to git us all bye for the next year."

Chicken and Goosey agreed. They all three spit on the sand some, kicking a few of the dried cow pies there in the cow pens.

Lochy Foxx's office was in the back of the Foxx County Bank. They siddled in at the front desk and told the gal at the front that they needed to see Lochy. She said, "Y'all'll have to wait a bit—he's finishin' up his talk to the Dale Carnegie Course. He's talkin' about how to chew tobacco at weddin's and such. He'll only be a minute."

They all sat down on the leather couch there in the lobby. Chicken took his hat off, holding it in his lap. Skinny licked her hand and mashed his cowlick down some. Somebody dropped a pencil, causing Goosey to jump and whir around to see whut is was that made the noise. Chicken growled at her. She sat down beside him. Her knuckles turned white as she grabbed a handful of his britches leg. At least she didn't cuss this time.

In a little while, the doors of the conference room opened and out comes an assortment of fine fat bidnessmen. They wuz smokin' cigars, laughing and shaking hands between themselves. Lochy Foxx saw that he had people waiting, so's he excused hisself and walked over to the customers. "How y'all doin'?" he asked as he stuck out his hand to Chicken.

"Fine," said Chicken. Lochy shook Skinny and Goosey's hand, but he kinda stood back a little from Skinny. He still remembered his was the last tooth she knocked out in the eighth grade. "Whut can I do fer you all? he asked.

"We mean to find out if'n we can borrie some money to tide us over this year. I'm sure you know the sky's fallin' in on us with the low cow prices and all," said Chicken.

"Yeah, it's bin a tough year so far," said Lochy, "Let's step into my office." He led them back to the back of the bank and they went into a room not much bigger than a broom closet. It had two straight-backed chairs and a five-gallon lard can in front of his desk. Lochy sat behind his desk in a black and white steer-hide chair. There were piles of papers, two deer heads mounted on the wall, one raggedy stuffed bobcat and a wood carving of a quail on his desk. He rolled a stale cigar and eyed them carefully. Lochy Foxx weren't much to look at but, as they say, he smelled like money.

They sat and explained their plight. Times were hard for all three of them. They owned the property next to his, each having about a section of land. That amounted to about 1800 acres between them. Lochy Foxx had about three sections, too.

Chicken said, "If the sky keeps fallin', we'll be ruined. We got to have money to make it 'til cow prices improve. We got to buy some hay, grass seed, horse feed, vaccines, worm and fluke medicine, and some fertilizer for the pastures." Skinny and Goosey agreed with Chicken.

Lochy Foxx turned sideways in his chair and listened with his fingers tented under his nose. After they finished tellin' him about all their plans for their ranches, he said, "I tell you whut I'm gonna do. I'll personally loan you the money—$20,000 each—for one year. Lets' see... today's date is September 15th. Y'all will have to pay it all back by noon on that day a year from now and the interest will be 5%, due at payoff. All you have to do is give me the deeds to your ranches to hold for collateral 'til the note's paid back. How's that suit you all?"

They looked at each other, Goosey swallowin' real loud, and then they all agreed by nods and handshakes. Lochy grinned like a possum eatin' a sour orange. "Wuz he up to something?" thought Chicken.

Lochy Foxx said, "Pick up the money here in the morning at 9:00. Okay?" They agreed and left the bank. All the way back to the ranches, Chicken kept thinkin' about that grin he had seen on Lochy's face. He'd seen it a time or two when they played cards. Lochy only grinned when he had the best hand or had you in his sights. Whut wuz he up to?

They gave Lochy their deeds to hold, signed the loan papers and picked up the money the next morning. It took the gal 30 minutes to count it all out in three piles of $20,000 each. For two days at the ranch they sat and talked over coffee about whut Lochy wuz up to.

Skinny said, "I don't trust him—never did and never will. But the sky is fallin' in on us." Goosey

36

agreed, recollecting he was one of the worst offend-
ers about goosing her up the slide.

Chicken said, "I don't either. We have to play our
cards close to our chests on this deal." They all took
turns spitting in the fireplace.

"Whut you reckon's the best place to start?" asked
Goosey.

"How 'bout we all write down all the ways we can
make some money off'n our ranches," said Skinny.

"Right! The girls said. They took turns spitting in
the fireplace again.

Chicken said, "I warn y'all—Lochy will hold us
to the penny. We have to lay $63,000 on his desk by
noon on the 15th of September come next year. The
more I think on it, the more uneasy I git."

So they thought and thought about how to make
money. They had to come up with $21,000 each by
next September 15th. So they figured and figured.
Finally, Chicken says, "I think we can go through our
cows and pick out the ones that ain't gonna calve.
We could sell them first because winter is comin' and
they won't make any money as dry cows. The sky may
fall in on us when we sell, but we'll have some money
to use for other things. Why couldn't we sort the cows
into groups so that we know who will calve and when?
We'll have to get the vet to help us, but it'll make
some money in the long run. Then I think we need
to call that woodcutter over by the sawmill. He might
want to cut pulpwood off our ranches. It won't hurt
anything cause they only want the small stuff. We best

leave some rough areas for the cows to calve in—out of the wind and all." It was agreed.

Goosey spoke up, "Whut about havin' that company come in and pull out the old lighterd pine stumps? They say they can make TNT or somethin' out of them."

"Whut if we sort the cows so that the heavy calvers are in a group," said Skinny, "That way we'll have 'em where we can help deliver any that have trouble." That was another good idea.

"You know, I jus' heard that if we put in some Brahma bulls, we'd get some tough hearty calves. Whut about that?" said Chicken. Good idea.

"I thought we might plant some clover in my marsh," said Skinny, "If y'all would plant some Pangola and Coastal Bermudagrass, we could open the gates and rotate the cattle. It means we'd have to mix herds, but they're all branded and ear marked so we could sort them later."

That too seemed like a good idea. Chicken said, "I think we could sell some small cabbage palms to those fellas that sell them up North. They cut out the hearts and call 'em "hearts of palm" up there. And, why not get a beeman out to out places to set up hives for honey?" A round of spitting in the fireplace followed a chorus of "Yeahs" and "'Spect sos."

So they set to. They worked from daylight 'til dark—"cain't see 'til cain't see." They got up all their cows and went through them with the vet, looking for culls and cows without calves. The vet selected the ones he called "open" an' they took them to market. The ones left were calvers—some soon calvers, others would calve late in the spring. They sorted them so they could keep close watch on the ones who would calve early in the year. The pulp wooders came, the beeman sat up his hives, and the cabbage palm cutters came and removed a thousand small cabbage palms. The lighterd stump trucks ran day and night as they removed the pine stumps that were made of condensed sap. In the winter, they planted clover on Skinny's marsh. It grew out lush in the spring. The Pangola and Bermuda grass sprigs went in the ground on schedule, and fertilizer made 'um stand tall.

That next spring the money just poured in. The beeman gave them honey, which they sold in town, the cabbage cutters dropped off a sack full of money, the pulpwooders and stump haulers sent checks, which they cashed into real money, and the cow sales added to the piles. Chicken, Skinny and Goosey put the money in big fruit jars and lard cans. They used the little Crisco cans, the gallon sized ones and the big five gallon ones like they use at the Twin Oaks Café—you know, that's tha head skin down near the lake. They buried them all around their cabins. They had holes everywher'! It looked like a army of gopher turtles and cur dog puppies had come through there. They didn't bother to count it. They jus' figured it'd take a bunch of it.

They ate swamp cabbage, guavas, oranges, wild pork, venison, gator tail, quail, dove, and squirrel to save on grocery bills. In the garden, Skinny raised greens and onions. Goosey planted some okra and Chicken grew corn. They didn't have to buy hay that winter since the ol' dry cows were gone. They had plenty of pasture. The cows were fatter'n town dogs. The vet had helped them keep only the cows with calves. They had a bumper crop of new calves that spring. The crossbred Brahmas were tough, hardy and meaner than snakes. They could kick the taste out'n yer mouth. But they grew good. Chicken began to smell money when he looked at them.

Lochy Foxx started coming around. He kept an eye on the operations. He indicated that he thought they'd never make the payoff on time. He asked a lot of question about cow numbers, and income off'n the stumps sales and such. He sure was curious about it all, thought Chicken. Chicken kept saying that he knew the sky was fallin'. Skinny and Goosey jus' avoided Lochy Foxx when they could. It got so that Lochy came by every week in August. Chicken figured he was planning to move in on the ranches as soon as possible. After all, he owned the three sections jus' next to theirs.

Time came near for the payoff. Chicken Little, Skinny Penny and Goosey Lucy dug up all the fruit jars and lard cans, putting them in the back of Chicken's truck. Off to town they went. At the bank, at 8:00 sharp, they started bringin' in cans full of coins and bills. They sat them on Lochy Foxx's desk. Sand fell off most of them. A limb-hit nephew of Lochy's got the broom and swept up the dirty sand. Lochy just growled at him when he got in the way. He had one of his counter girls start counting it. They opened cans and counted and counted and counted—for three hours they counted and piled the money.

At about 11:35, jus' before the deadline, Lochy grinned and said, "Well, boys and girls, it looks like y'all are gonna be short by $6,243.82. Heh, heh, I guess y'all will have to forfeit your ranches," he said as he patted the deeds. The three sat real stunned like as the news sunk in. Had they forgot a can?

After a long silence while everyone wuz thinkin', Goosey jumped up and ran in a tite circle, shouting and screamin' somethin' in some foreign language. They tried to calm her down some. One of the girls brought her a glass of water. They sat her down, fanning her and telling her to take it easy.

She finally got herself together some, studderin', "I got s-s-some money I forgot a-about! I opened one of them new fangled c-c-checkin' accounts here at the b-b-b-bank—I d-don't know how much I got in it!"

So ol' Chicken told the gal behind the counter to bring a check for Goosey. She was so excited to remember that she'd done such a thing. Lochy was a little put out by the news—he'd already started counting his chickens before they hatched, it seems. In his mind, he'd cut the fences and already let his cattle in on their grass.

So Goosey wrote and wrote on the check. She'd pause and think. She'd write a bit, get up, shout, circle around the counter, returning to write a bit more. It was nigh on to ten minutes till noon on the 15th of September when Goosey handed the Foxx County Bank check to Lochy Foxx, President thereof. The check was a work of art. On it she had drawn a cartoon picture of little Lochy as her fist hit him in the eighth grade. A tooth was flyin' off into the air. On one other corner, she'd drawn Goosey slapping Lochy after he'd goosed her on the slide at school. At the bottom she'd drawn Chicken Little grinning an evil grin at Lochy at a card game, while he wuz layin' down a royal flush on the table.

The office girls just clapped in glee, Lochy just grumbled under his breath, shoving the deeds over to them. Chicken Little, Skinny Penny and Goosey Luck hooted out and slapped the table. The stacks of coins and money fell to the floor as they did it.

Goosey asked, "Have I got anymore in the bank?" The gal behind the counter checked. She said, "Why yes!! You have another $21,294.36!" Goosey said, "I'll take it in cash—now, please." They all hooted again. Mad Lochy up and left the room, slammin' his office door. Chicken grabbed the deeds and they pulled out for Padgett's Drugstore for a root beer.

Things settled down some. Goosey spilt the money between them all. The routine returned for the three—until Chicken sold some more cows the following late summer. The cow price was low again.

He drove his ol' raggedy truck down to Padgett's Drugstore. There at the soda fountain sat Skinny Penny and Goosey Lucy. Chicken Little came up and sat down beside them at an open stool.

He cocked his hat back on his head saying, "The sky's fallin' in!"

Skinny said, "Her' we go agin!"

Goosey jumped, swatted at an imaginary fly and said, "Bark! Bark!"

CHAPTER SIX

THE SLEEPIN' BEAUTY

Oncst upon a time there was a kingdom 'bout a day's ride from here. I don't know whut y'all have heard 'bout this story, but here's my take on it. There was a king and queen and they had them a little princess there. Oh, she was a beautiful sight to behold! But she kinda ran things her own way it seems. At times, she was a regular wild woman of Borneo. Some say she wuz crazier than a outhouse rat, but she had her own truck, the nicest cloths and her pick of all the local boy princes. Wellsir, one day she up and married one of them. Now it soon came to lite that this here marriage was doomed to fail. The boy prince didn't play the game too well. He kept on hog huntin', fishin' and goin' to buckouts with the other princes. Durin' these buckouts, he learned to drink ale and such. Lots of other princess' came to these parties, too. There was always wenchin', laughin', dancin', fightin' and so forth at these affairs. This didn't suit his bride the princess queen—she wanted to pretty much run the whole show it seems. So ther' wuz all kinds of malcontent and disturbance in the whole kingdom.

The king and queen didn't have any idea whut to do with her. She up an' left the prince high and dry. She had had a little princess by the fella, so she up and flew the coup with her and everythin' that weren't tied down. The prince come home to find the trailer purty much stripped of anythin' of worth. His saddle and spurs, Sunday hat, silver rodeo belt buckle, kangaroo skin boots and his pocket pistol wuz all gone. All that wuz left wuz a ol' black an' white television, some canned peaches and a note. The note read: "I wuz here and you wadn't... Now I ain't and you are." This made little sense to him—but it wuz the way things had gone the whole of the marriage. I don't think the poor fella really knew whut to do about this whole affair—after all, he wuz jus an ol' country prince. So he redoubled his efforts at the buckout circuit and rodeoin', leaving the trailer behind. The last time I saw him he wuz cuttin' a cabbage in the woods on Peace River.

The princess re-established her rule in the family of the king and queen. She flitted around the kingdom like a wren in a party hat. All the princes figured they'd have a shot at her but she kept cool. All the other local princesses knew she was a tough cookie, so they didn't mess with her much.

About two years later a handsome prince moved into the neighboring kingdom. He sat up his own kingdom there under a benevolent king. He got him a new truck, and set about making gold and silver. He prospered by hard work and good investment. For instance, one time he planted a dime's worth of turnip seed and made 1000% on his investment. Everythin' he touched seemed to prosper. His reputation spread. He was known as a good catch by all the princesses around these parts.

So one day the neighborin' kingdom decided to have a fair to raise gold and silver for a worthy cause. There wuz poor people around and they needed cloths, grits, side meat, beans and coffee. So the ministers of the fair decided to have a prince-for-a-date auction. Course, the idea wuz to let the local princesses bid on bachelor princes and give the purse to the poor people.

The big day arrived. People from as far away as 35 miles came to the fair. They all gathered up at the barn and the frolic began. There wuz jams and jellies, biscuits and cookies, swamp cabbage and ribs and other delights. The peak of the affair was the auction of the princes, includin' the prince that ain't from around here, for dates to the gals that wer' highest bidders. All the princesses gathered around. Many of them wuz already married and could not participate. They jus wanted to watch. But the unmarried ones flocked in like cow herons on fresh-plowed pasture. The fair organizers put the ten princes in big boxes and put bows on them. Now the prince that wadn't from around here wuz in the big box with a red bow. Word got around that he wuz in that box. Biddin'

47

went along without a hitch until they came to the red bow box. The princess from the neighborin' kingdom knew that he wuz there and decided that she wuz goin' to git him at any price—whatever it took. Biddin' started as usual but it wuz soon apparent that she would not be denied this little beautiful prince. Bids grew higher and higher, more and more time went into the biddin' and finally all the princesses dropped by the wayside. She won the bid. The red bow wuz taken off and inside the little purty prince that wadn't from around here wuz fast asleep. He'd had a day of hard work and excitement—he was as tired as a wormy yearling. The princess leaned over and kissed him on the lips. He awoke with a start and realized that he'd been won by the princess from afar. No one knows what he thought at that moment. Wuz he in for a ride? Wuz he grabbin' a bull by the tail? Or wuz the bull grabbin' him by the tail? Truth is, she had big plans for him. Jus' like a Louis L'Amour tale, he wuz soon to discover that she wuz the Queen and he would always be a prince.

That wuz the beginnin' of a wild ol' time. They went to rodeos, cookouts, buckouts, picnics, trips to the beach and such. She decided that they wuz to marry. He wuz just along for the ride it seems. He begin to look puny, sickly and worn out. He looked like an earthworm with his guts slung out. We tried to fatten him up, but he jus' had too much goin' on. We wormed him, fed him lots of corn and fried foods, but he jus' couldn't gain weight. He has this haggard look about him—though ther' seemed to be a smile on his face most of the time. They married some twelve months later at a castle north of both their kingdoms. She moved into his kingdom and started takin' over.

The benevolent king tolerated her but it caused consternation among his subjects and his queen. It soon became apparent that she wuz up to no good. In her aim to set up a kingdom within the kingdom of the benevolent king, she created nuthin' but confusion and contention. The new marriage of the beautiful prince who ain't from around here and the princess queen from afar made life hard for the subjects of the benevolent king. He began to work things within his kingdom that would shut down the plans for takeover by this new queen and sleeping prince who wadn't from around here. The prince and princess figured that they could indeed establish their own kingdom. They packed their accumulated wealth and moved to a place far, far away. He built a castle there and they lived happily, albeit with bluster, ever after.

Tales still circulate among the local folk, of the two kingdoms, about the headstrong Queen-princess and the sleeping beauty bachelor prince in the box with a red bow. Everyone seemed to let out a sigh of relief when they moved. They come back to the kingdoms occasionally, startin' up some activities and confusion. But she still is the Queen and he tha' sleepin' beautiful prince from the box with a red bow.

CHAPTER SEVEN

RUSSELL STILT'S SKIN

Now rite off, I know whut yer thinkin'! But ya got it all wrong! This ain't no story 'bout some knotty nosed, short-legged fella with a squeaky voice, runnin' around in the woods in a pointy hat, tryin' to get some gal to throw her twenty-foot long wig out the winder of her daddy's house or 'bout her makin' gold out of Bermudagrass hay or such as that. Nosir! This is the true version as it wer told to me when I wuz no taller than a little turkey hen. I don't know where that other fella got his version of the story he calls Rumpelstiltskin—his'n is before my time.

The Stilt family wuz all raised around Clearwater, way back there when it a little town. Why, the roads were still sand and shell then and they used old fish heads to fertilize the orange groves—that's how long ago it wuz. Anyways, the Stilts were a fine bunch of people. There wuz only Mama and Papa and the two kids, Russell and Sister. Now Sister had a real fine name but I forgot it. Everybody always called her Sister. She never got flustered with much, stayed real quiet most of the time. She didn't complain when Russell gave her the puppy's worm pills. The fact is, she slicked off, gained weight and her hair got plum glossy after that.

Russell Stilt was a real independent sort. At twelve years old, he'd take to the woods after school on Fridays. He'd come home, gather up four or five shotgun shells, some rice, some dried lima beans, a jacket, and a bedroll of some kind. Off he'd go into the deep woods on the edge of Clearwater. Ya see, then, Clearwater was a settlement—it weren't much wider than a big palmetto patch then. Mama never thought anythin' of it. He always come home on Sunday nite. Mama and Daddy spoke French but Russell and Sister never spoke it much, but maybe a little at the dinner table. Anyways, Russell grew up in the woods. He could hunt, fish, trap, skin, trade and cook. He met a man in the woods named Joe. Joe wuz half-Seminole and wise to the woods. Joe taught him everythin' he knew but Russell wuz quick to pick up new stuff, too.

Russell wuz ah plum enterprisin' fella. He used to buy Cuban bananas at the pier in Tampa, sellin' them by hangin' them on a tree limb in the town square, "5 cents for a bunch—Leave the money in the cigar box," his sign said. He did okay in that. He noticed the bicyclers came every winter. So he sat up a fried squirrel stand near a crossroads. The sign said, "Fried Squirrel—All you want, 5 cents! Leave money in the cigar box." He did good there, too—until they started stealin' his squirrel. He made a deal with the local feed store owner to kill out his rats for him. Under the feed store, there lived a whole passel of rats—Russell figured he'd break the cyclers from stealing his squirrel. You could hear the .22 balls rickashayin' off the boards as he cleaned 'er out of big fine fat rats.

He went home, got a skillet and some lard and fried up a bait of fresh skinned rats. He put them in the pan, set up his sign, like always. Sure enough, the bicyclers stole his fried rats, not leavin' any money. The next day, he put up a sign that said, "We sure wish to thank you bicyclers for helpin' us clean out the rats at the feed store." They never come back that way again. He went back to supplin' fried squirrel for the locals.

Anyway, time went on and Russell Stilt grew into a fine young man. His papa wuz a schoolteacher an' encouraged Russell to go to college. Now this weren't no common thing, 'cause few people went to college from his town, but Russell figured that might just give him an edge.

Let me take a round-about way of tellin' you about his college. Most folks don't know a thing about the area where the college was built, but here goes. Way back in 1817 there wuz a Timucuan Village in the northern central region of Florida. Now, the Timucua wer' tha' original Native Americans who populated the northern part of Florida and a little of the southern part of Georgia. The old records tell us they took up from 19,000 to 20,000 square miles. It was a big area and some claim there were as many as thirty-five chiefs ruling the various tribes. In 1513, the Spanish showed up and the Timucuan wuz probably the ones who met them. It was many years later, in 1565, when the Spanish built a fort and town named St. Augustine. But several things happened. During that period—things that would destroy the Timucua. Firstly, they never organized any resistance to the newcomers, but often fought amonst themselves. Most devastatin' was their lack of immunity to the newcomers' diseases.

The differences between tha' natives an' tha' Spaniards were great. The native populations were not concerned about land ownership. They lived "off the land" an' defended their huntin' territories against other tribe's invasions. These Europeans wanted to own land, settle and farm it; they had an entirely different view of land. This created a lot of hard feelings between the newcomers and tha' native tribes. Tha' natives saw nothin' wrong with killing anyone intrudin' on their tribe's areas. 'Course, tha' newcomers retaliated. Wars and skirmishes wer' frequent. Over the period from 1513 to1700 the numbers of Timucua dwindled from perhaps as many as 200,000, down to 1000. As far as I can tell, the Timucua were extinct by the 1800's.

Many people overlook tha' fact that many Native American tribes were in constant warfare with other tribes, so some tribes "joined" with the Europeans to war against their "traditional tribal enemies". Same thing happened in South America when the Spanish conquered that region. I specultate that without the help of willing natives, the Europeans might have had a tough time defeating the vast number of dominant tribes.

Now all that leads to what I'm goin' to tell you about the college Russell enrolled in. The original name for the area wuz "Hogtown". It wuz once a Timucuan Indian village which in 1824 had a population of fourteen. Hogtown was one of the earliest settlements in Alachua County.

In tha' late 1820's Hogtown became a white settlement as American pioneers moved in an' occupied the land formerly inhabited by Seminoles, who had, by this time, had been removed by the terms of a treaty.

During the Second Seminole War from 1835-1842, a settler's fort was built at the Hogtown settlement near this site. Tha' place was then called "Fort Hogtown". It wuz one of more than a dozen forts in the area. Twelve years later the town of "Gainesville" was founded on a site located a few miles east of Ft. Hogtown. A proposed railroad was by-passing a city north of Gainesville so the area residents voted to create a new town on the railroad line and make it tha' county seat. Tha' new town was founded on September 6, 1853, and wuz called "Gainesville", named in honor of Seminole Indian War General Edmund P. Gaines. Tha' city wuz growin' in size an' prosperity when, in 1906, the University of Florida began operations on land west of the city. How close to the old Ft. Hogtown site, I don't rightly know, but I 'spect most of the graduates of this fine institution would rather not talk about it.

Russel rode in a Model T Ford to college, through Payne's Prairie—it used to be a big lake 'til a big sink-hole formed in one end. All the water just flowed out one day, leavin' a paddle wheel boat high and dry. So Russell enrolled in the college at Ft. Hogtown.

He graduated from the college with a degree in agriculture. You ever hear of "Cum Laude"? That means, "with honors," I think. Russell graduated with "Oh Lordy." He learned the difference between Tangelos and Page, Hamlin and Valencia oranges and between Marsh and Ruby Red grapefruits at the college.

He got his sheepskin diploma in June of 1922. It wuz a good time to be a college graduate in ol' Florida. Papa called it, "Russell Stilt's Skin." That's where the name of the story comes from. It weren't long after that that the depression hit. Russell didn't seem to be affected by it since he gardened and lived off the woods game. He bought a feed store, selling it later at a profit. He started a tree and ornamental nursery, sold that for a profit, too. His idea wuz that you'd never go broke makin' a profit and to always let the other man make a nickel off the deal. He cleared ten acres for a man once for the deed to the adjacent ten acres as payment. Highway 19 came right through the middle of it—even before he'd cleared it. This put him on the map as far as money is concerned.

He got a job with the government after that in an agriculture program after the big war. It wuz to help farmers get loans to grow food for people. He traveled all around ol' Florida—way before there wuz fences and good roads. But he learned a lot about the country, and whut to do and not do in agriculture. Once day he come across a piece of property that had a lot of potential. He and another fella bought it, sub-divided it for sale to git the parts they wanted most. It wuz a good place, with hammocks, marshes, piney woods and bays. An ol' railroad went through the heart of it—you know the one that went from New Smyrna to Okeechobee?

Wellsir, he set to developin' the ranch. It had some native cattle on it when he bought it. He brought in some good breedin' sires and started to get better calves. By this time, he had such a good reputation, he could call the banker and tell him to put $50,000 in his account and that he'd pay him later—the deal wuz made on the telephone! He thought and thought about whut he could do to make money to pay off the loans and for operation costs. He always said, "It don't hurt to borrow money if you have more than one way to pay it back." After studyin' on it for days and weeks, he decided that he could grow citrus there. It'd never been done and everyone thought he wuz losin' his mind in doin' it. But he knew it could be done. By then he had a son also named, Russell.

Everybody called him Russ, so's they wouldn't git the two of 'em confused.

They put in the groves by plantin' the trees in rows, jus like they did at Indian River, near Ft. Pierce. But the difference wuz that he put the trees in so they could water them in dry times on shallow beds and let the water flow out in deep ditches during the wet times. If'n I had the time, I'd draw you a picture of how they done it. He planted Hamlin orange trees. Now these oranges come ripe about early fall. The idea wuz to get the fruit off the trees before the winter freezes and the hurricanes hit. It worked good, too, in beatin' everyone else to the market. In fact, it worked reel good.

So that wuz the start of a great thing. He cleared land, leavin' places for the wildlife, and he grew cattle and citrus. The place took off and grew and grew. He had sons and daughters and grandchildren that run behind his jeep with his dogs for years and years. Today, sum sixty-five years later, that ranch is a sight to behold. It all comes back to Russell Stilt's Skin—that sheep-skin diploma he got at the college at Ft. Hogtown. Course, character had a lot to do with it, too. Now that's the true story as I heard it when I wuz as little as a green tree frog.

CHAPTER EIGHT

THE THREE LITTLE CRACKER PIGS

Now I don't know whut you heard before 'bout this story. I first heard it in its true form many years ago. I wuz a little lad when it were told to me. There wuz these three little cracker pigs born in the woods one time. The hog hunter's came through one day and caught their mama and papa. They also caught several of their brothers and sisters. They mite near wiped out the whole bunch of 'em, 'septin' the three littlest ones.

"I swan," said Phyleaux, "I never 'spected to be on our own so early. I sure do miss Mama and Papa."

"Tell me 'bout it," said Claude.

"Yep," said Sy, "Dat wuz plum boogerin' ta me—I 'till have nitemares 'bout them dogs that tum with 'um."

"Don't it jus' chap yer lips?" said Phyleaux.

"Shur does," agreed Claude.

"Uh-huh!" said Sy, "Dat really trows hair on da cake, don't it?"

The three little cracker pigs started makin' their way in the wild new world of the Florida backwoods. They'd root here and there, amble along, lookin' for grubs, acorns and anythin' that could be 'et. They were after all little fellas and needed plenty of groceries to make it. Why Claude even tried to eat a frog onsct—he like' to have never caught it—it kept hoppin' and squirmin' around. He finally trapped him in a shallow gopher hole. He said it wadn't much good for all the work it took to catch 'em. They each tried to eat a gopher tortoise once—that wuz a sight! The old gopher just sucked back in his shell and out-waited them. They quit him purty fast since he wuz way too much trouble. Anyways they dauddled around the pastures and marshes, always lookin' for somethin to eat. Fact is they spent all their time lookin' for food.

One time they saw a truck drivin' out in a pasture. They hid in the tall grass and watched. The man pulled up to a little tiny buildin' of sorts and proceeded to unload some cow feed. The three little pigs watched close. Wuz this somethin' to eat? After a time, the man stopped, got off the bed of the truck and lite whut appeared to them as a white stick. The fella jus' sit there on the tailgate and looked all around. Little puffs of smoke came from around his head.

"Fire! Fire! cried Sy. They got all excited and ran around a bit. They stopped a little ways off and looked back.

"The danged fool ain't runnin' away," said Claude.

"Maybe it ain't bad," said Phyleaux.

They settled back in the grass to watch. After a time, the man gets in the truck and drives off.

"Whut wuz that all about?" said Claude. Sy said he thought they ought to go close and investigate. They approached real quite like. Sy went to gruntin' some—all nervous like. The others told him to be quiet.

Wellsir, the closer they got, the better it smelled. It smelled like molasses! They went closer. Finally, Sy eased up and looked around. There wuz some cow feed spilt on the ground. He tried a taste. It wuz dood to him—uh-huh! The other two joined him and ate the spilt feed. Claude figured a way to git into the little trough and began to load up on the sweet feed. That's how he got his nickname, Cowboy Claude. They always laughed about that. Anyways, they ate their fill and moved on. This got to be a regular event in their little world. They'd watch for the man and his truck. Oh, they'd run off a little ways when they saw him but they'd always come back onsct he wuz gone. With all the grubs, ripe citrus, acorns, frogs, clover, berries and the sweet feed, they grew into nice sized shoats—a little on the thin side but they were growin'.

One day on one of their jaunts Sy caught the flicker of a dark shadow crossin' the trail behind them. He "woofed" an alarm to the others. Phyleaux came up close and they watched for the longest time before they saw it again. It wuz a panther! It wuz trailin' them! Off they went like shot out of a cannon, straight for the thick palmetto patch 'bout a hundred yards ahead of them. They squirmed, crawled, dug under and climbed the jumble of roots until they were smack dab in the middle of the thickest palmetto patch you ever saw.

Mr. Panther came up. He walked all around the patch. He said, "Come on out, boys, I know yer in there."

"No way," sez Claude, "We ain't comin' out!"

Mr. Panther sez, "Now, boys, y'all know ther' ain't no way that y'all can git away from a panther. Come on out and save yerselves some worry time—I'll only eat one of you."

"Uh-uh," said Sy, "We'uns is 'tayin' rite here."

Mr. Panther sez, "I do declare, y'all are plum saucy." After walkin' all around the palmetto patch, Mr. Panther said, "I 'spect I'll ease on down by the woods, I saw a fawn down there that I could eat."

"Dood idea," said Sy.

Mr. Panther had no plan on leavin' such a delicacy as piglet. But he made a show of leavin', whistlin' and singin' real loud at times the Battle Hymn of the Republic as he walked a ways from the patch. Sy wuz more than a little wary. He looked at his brothers with a nervous look. Phyleaux and Claude moved out to the edge of the patch to see wher' the panther went. Sure enough, they glimpsed him about three hundred yards away on little bank of dirt.

They looked around for an escape. "Now, if we stay on the other side of the patch, outa sight, stayin' in the grass for about thirty yards, we can git to that little dry drainage ditch. It runs to the woods. There we mite be able to slip away for Mr. Panther.," said Phyleaux.

Nervous swallers could be heard among the trio. Finally, Claude made a break for it. The other two joined him and they all then slipped to the ditch, down the ditch and into the woods. They run like the wind before a hurricane. Their little ears were jus' flappin' in the breeze and their legs were a blur as they run.

Somehow, they slipped the panther. It could have been they ran near the groves where the men wuz sprayin' the orange trees. It did smell bad, too. They jus' seemed to know that panthers don't like people much—they avoided them ever' chancst they got. Into the deep, deep woods they ran. Back into brambles, bushes, briars and thick underbrush they went. They come to a bayhead. It wuz a marshy swamp. Back in the middle of it wuz a little high place that wadn't under the water. The mucky mud and water would act like a barrier of sorts, keepin' them a little safer from Mr. Panther. They knew he'd come after them—it wuz jus' a matter of time. All three of the little pigs had to root and root to git in this dense place. But once it, they had a little island all to themselves. They rested all that day and the next. But they all got hungry. They had to go out for food. So they decided to split up and search. They could go back to the cow feeder but they knew it would be watched.

So for days they lived undisturbed there in their little island in the bayhead. But one day, Sy come runnin' in and yelled, "Tha panther's comin'! He's rite behind me!"

Sure enough, Mr. Panther had trailed Sy to their lair. They all got in a tight bunch in the middle. They rooted and crawled under the thickest brush there. Mr. Panther came. He circled the bayhead, smellin' the air. He squalled out like a wild woman in plum frustration—at being so close to tasty pigs but them bein' so hard to git to. He called out, "I sees y'all have a new home. This one is a bit better. Y'all know how much I hate to get my feet muddy. But y'all will have to come out sometime. I'll be waitin'. Come on out and save two of yourselves from bein' scared all the time."

Claude spoke up, sayin', "You'll get plum titejawed if'n you wait on us—we ain't comin' out for nuthin'." Mr. Panther screamed his anger. He paced and paced, circled and circled. He grew madder than a dirt dauber in a empty tin can. The boys jus' settled down for the wait. The thing they had goin' for them wuz tha panther kept squallin' out when he wuz mad. That's the way they knew where he wuz. He got on the far side of the little swamp, where ther' wuz an over-flow creek going out. They figured that'd be all the break they'd git.

Off they went, helter-skelter, elbow over teacup, through the swamp, out the woods and toward the big lake. They ran and ran and ran. Ever now and agin, they'd stop and listen. Onsct the screamin' stopped, they knew the panther wuz on their trail. He wuz fast, mean and could trail a walkin' spider from his three-day old tracks. They'd stop and listen some. The squallin' had stopped. They knew they wer' in deep trouble. On and one they ran, as fast as their little legs would go.

Now I don't know if y'all know how fast the weather can change sometimes. There wuz a black scum of clouds in the northwestern sky. It come up durin the day and things were getting' darker as the day went on. The trees and grass begin to tussle some. The wind picked up in little fits at first, turnin' into real blusters. The little pigs were desperate for a safe place to hide. They had panicked a little since they had run out in the open. As they say in these parts, "Their mules wuz scared." They stopped to rest on a hillock. This allowed them to look back at the marsh. They watched real close for the shadow of the panther. The wind blew hard, little spits of rain hit their faces and backs. Birds flew toward roosts known only to them. The sawgrass swished in the gusts. A storm wuz a'comin'.

"There!" squealed Claude, "He's a'comin'!" Sure 'nough, here come Mr. Panther jus' joggin' along, sniffin' the ground where's the little pigs had trotted. He'd stop ever now and agin, look around, as if he wuz not sure where he wuz. The three little cracker pigs took to the grass, runnin' for all they wuz worth. Down behind the dyke they went, tail over the dashboard. They slipped under a fence, heading down a little lane where the grass wuz rubbed into little patches of bare sand. It were a road of some kind, but they wuz in a panic—they had a hungry panther on their tails and he wuz comin' steady.

Sy wuz the first to see it. A little shack on pilings sat before them. It had a couple of little cur dog puppies playin' in the yard of it. An old Model T truck that had been rode hard and put up wet wuz sitting under a tall myrtle tree. A woodpile wuz just off the porch. A fine guava tree was out behind, near a little barn. The place looked empty. A couple of nervous chickens were bug huntin' in the back of it, lookin' at the sky and havin' their feathers ruffled by the wind.

Claude said, "Make for it—git under the porch!" They made it to the shack just as a terrible toad stranglin' storm rain come upon it. The grass blew flat, the myrtles were upset a mite, and little bits of leaves and grasses flew by in the gusts. The chickens darted for the little barn and the puppies got up next to the front door on the porch. They kinda hunkered down there. The storm wuz a terrible thing. The rain hit in thick sheets on the little tin roof of the shack and the pigs jus' knew it'd blow down. It held together though, how they didn't know.

They crawled deep under the shack back to the middle of it where there was a small square brick wall of sorts. Somehow the bricks were warm. They jostled each other a bit, tryin' to git close to the bricks. They were cold and wet. They didn't know about foundations of fireplaces. All they knew wuz those warm bricks really felt good to three tired, scared little cracker pigs. The storm blew and blew. The air got cool. It didn't seem to wanna let up. Dark came early that day. The rain continued on into the night. The pigs hunkered down for a long blow. Did that panther lurk like a huntin' gator right outside? Wuz it waitin' for them to show their faces in the night? Which one would be the dinner of the mad beast? They didn't know. All they knew wuz that he'd be madder than ever if'n he wuz wet and he surely wuz, out in this weather. If weren't fit for panthers (or pigs, for that matter). They worried some about whut they'd do once the storm wuz over. But it kept on blowing rain for the longest time.

They heard a bump in the night. Somethin' stirred. There wuz a scrape on the wood in the night as black as pitch. They figured they best lay quiet as possible—they didn't see any other way to go about it. Wuz that panther upon them? Wuz he in the house? The noises grew louder. There wuz a prying sound, one like a board creekin' above them. And all of a sudden, above them a board wuz pulled back and a old man's face appeared in the hole. He wuz holdin' a kerosene lantern, peerin' down on them from above. This man had a sun burned jaw. His beard wuz several days thick. He had an ol' straw cowboy hat just like the man who put out the cow feed they liked so much. There were deep lined wrinkles in his chin and cheeks. His skin wuz all leathery brown. He sure wuz ugly to the pigs—but who were they to talk?

He said, "I wish you'd look! I got company on this rainy night. How you boys doin'?" He chuckled slightly. Then he laughed. "I know you boys, I seen you at the cow feeder. Yeah, y'all er the one's who bin stealin' cow feed. Yeah, that's you, ain't it, Claude? You're the whelp that likes to git in the trough." He laughed out loud. He left the hole, the light disappearin' a bit. He came back in a while and tossed somethin' down the hole. It landed with a flop-flop, jus' beside Phyleaux. The pigs were startled some, but then, jus' at they were about to panic, a wonderful aroma came to them all at once.

Sy said, "Look! It look like tum tind of food."

Claude eased over, careful to keep his eye on the man's face above him. He smelled it. "It sure smells good, boys," he grunted. He took a taste of it. Then he said, "Gather up, boys! It's good eatin'!" That wuz the first time they'd ever tasted grits, guava pie, swamp cabbage and big yellow lima beans.

Sy said, "Dis is dood ta me... Uh-huh!!" It really wuz good to all their little bellies that night.

Now the Raulersons had always lived around the big lake for nigh on to four generations, ever since old great-grand daddy Raulerson settled there back in the mid-1800s. He come there from Georgia before the time of the big war between the states some say.

Most folks around there knew them as good fishermen. But Earnest Raulerson had settled in this little shack not far from Lake Okeechobee. He built his house on pilings since the water often came up as high as his porch durin' the summer rains. He'd sit out a hurricane or two. But over all, he had a good spot for his house. He day worked for some of the other ranches around there. He'd been a tough man all his life. His wife died about ten years ago. He'd been alone but content to work here and there some, bunchin' and workin' cattle for others. He never had much store in material things. He had swamp cabbage, fresh fish and turtle, venison, turkey, and a garden. But he was a little lonely. These pigs were a sight to his old eyes. They were little and a bit on the puny side of things. How in the world they had come to be under his shack, he had no idea. The last time he heard noises under his shack, he'd pulled a board and threw a pan of hot water down there. Wellsir, that hot water fell in on a nest of skunks. You talk about a stink! Son! It wuz plum awful! He had to sleep out on the porch for two weeks in the mosquitoes until that stink settled down. He said, "After a week, you git kinda used to the smell." Anyways he looked this time before he poured hot water. There they were—three orphaned pigs. Might make a good relationship. After all they didn't talk much. He liked that idea.

So if you happened to drive down the hard road down by Lake Okeechobee about dark some weeks after that stormy day, you could often see a man sittin' on his porch. Two puppies would be playing, a few chickens would be rustlin' up bugs and three fat little pigs could be seen layin' in the yard under the guava tree. They all seemed content with their lives. They respected each other it seems. He'd talk to them and they'd grunt a bit back at him. They were good friends. Mr. Panther came by a few times. Ol' Man Raulerson shot his shotgun near him—jus' to let him know the pigs were his buddies. After just a few times, the panther got the idea. He moved on, plannin' to return to check on them ever so often. The pigs loved it there. This wuz a house that the panther couldn't take and Ol' Man Raulerson wuz their best friend. They'd run their last time from Mr. Panther.

If you want to see a sight, go by there on a Saturday afternoon. Most likely you'll see Ol' Man Raulerson sittin' in a tub on the front porch with soap foam all over his head. He'll be singin' a song about some far away place—a place he's never seen. In the yard the chickens will be doin' what chickens do. And, you'll likely see one or two pigs and a pup on the porch watchin' him take his bath. Life sure is good on the marshes of Lake Okeechobee.

It's funny how the least likely creatures become friends—who would have thought a lonely man, three pigs, two cracker puppies, four chickens and a hungry panther would form a friendship...

CHAPTER NINE

THE STORY OF THE GRINNIN' GOPHER

I know you ain't ever heard the story 'bout the little gopher turtle. I never heard anyone tell it 'sep my grandmamma. She told it for the truth. So here goes.

Oncst upon a time there was a little gopher turtle. He weren't much as land turtles go. He wadn't purty or anythin'. He jus' minded his own bidness. He'd git out and around some most every day. He'd eat grass and tender plants on these jaunts in the country. He'd built hisself quite a home in the ground. His hole went back into the earth some thirty feet. He'd come in from a hard day of foragin' and dig on it most every day. Every now and agin a armadillo would come in his hole. They were a mite touches about others in the same hole as they were. They'd usually leave when the gopher come home. Besides they worked the evenin' shift, while gopher worked days.

Late one day there was a terrible fire in the woods. It was dry. Lightening started it and the fire got rank in a hurry. Gopher pulled out, albeit a little slow, for

71

home. He arrived there to find that in his house wuz a baby rabbit, a piglet, a fox and a big ol' rattlesnake. He pushed hisself into the crowd. He said, "Well... I didn't... know... I wuz goin'... ta have... company."

The fox said, "Yeah, get used to it—the fire is rank out there! I seen ya workin' out in the pasture. I knew there'd be a hole nearby."

The rabbit said, "Yep, yep, yep... we gotta stay out the fire... yep, yep, yep. No doubt about it... we got to stay the night..."

The piglet snorted, saying, "We won't stay long," (snort, grunt), "It'll blow over within a couple of hours."

The big rattler said, "S-s-s-sure... we won't s-s-s-stay long-th-th-th-h-h."

Gopher said, "All... right... y'all can... stay...'til the... fire... is out."

The fire was really somethin'. It got into the palmettos and pines and like to have never quit. It wuz hotter than white-hot blazes of lightening. It was so intense it kicked up great clouds of black and gray smoke. The palmettos burnt to skinny stalks on gnarled burnt roots. Pine trees suffered the leaping flames, the lowest green needles scorched to a dull brown and the trunk bark turned to black. There was a muffled roar as the fire consumed all the grass, bushes and any creature that didn't escape. But they all kept to themselves in the gopher's hole, though it wuz a little tite quarters.

Night came. Gopher heard some unfamiliar sounds in the dark. The rabbit squeaked once, the piglet squealed, the fox gave a yip and the snake he never once heard. Come daylight only Gopher and Rattlesnake were left in the hole.

Gopher thought that this wuz plum peculiar. Wher' had everybody gone? He noticed that rattler was rather fat in the belly. He moved real slow, too. Gopher ast him, "Wher'… is… ever'…body?"

"S-s-s-s-sth-seems-s-s-s to me, s-s-s-s-sth…. they up an' left."

Gopher jus' knew that this here snake wuz lyin' outen his fangs. He watched him close. The rattler began to ease around some. The next thin' Gopher knew, he wuz blocked in the hole. Rattler grinned a plum evil grin. Now Gopher wadn't much on runnin'—fact is he couldn't run. He wuz more than a little upset at this situation.

Snake moved a little closer, sayin', "Gopher, s-s-s-sth-step over clos-s-s-ser to me, let me tell you a s-s-s-s-secret."

Now Gopher wuz a little smarter than everyone thought. He said, "I……. guess you……… plan to eat me……..too."

"Yes-s-s-s-sth," Snake said, "I s-s-s-spect yer right-s-s-s-sth."

"You ate….. everyone….. in here…… dent you?"

"No," said Snake, "Tha piglet ate the baby rabbit-sth, the fox-s-s-sth ate the piglet, and I ate tha fox-s-s-s-sth."

Gopher thought a minute and said, "I'll make….. you a bet…. If'n I win…… you…. will….. let me….. go… Howz….. that?"

"S-s-s-sths-ounds fair to me-s-s-sth," said Snake, coilin' a little tighter, getting ready to strike, Gopher thought.

Gopher swallered real loud and said, "I bet... you... cain't... eat yer rattlers...

"Oh, I can... s-s-sth," said Snake.

"Cain't," said Gopher.

Back and forth they bantered until finally Snake said, "Deal! Watch this-s-s-sth!" And he grabbed his tail and commenced to eat the rattlers.

Tha next thing you know, his mouth wuz full of his own tail! He started swallerin' his tail and his jaw crept up higher and higher on his body.

He kept goin' and goin' and finally, he jus' disappeared—he ate hisself up! Poof! He wuz gone! Gopher knew that snakes were bad about swallerin' anything they started eatin'.

He grinned, sayin', "Heh... heh...heh... That ... works... ever'... time."

Now that's the way she tol' it ta me. You don't believe me? Look real close at the next gopher turtle you see—he'll have a little smile on his face. Heh... heh... Heh-h-h.

CHAPTER TEN

DRINKIN' COFFEE

I 'spect you'll be plum googily-eyed when you hear this story. It ain't about some make-believe people. It's all about drinkin' coffee. You know how it is when we go to the woods an' build a fire and put on coffee? You know how the smoke smells and tha coals git reel hot? An' ther' so hot that when you poke 'em the poke-stick catches on fire? You remember the frogs—how they "wheir" and "ratchet" in the night? An' how we'd set then an' drink the cowboy coffee? That's jus' a way of life fer us crackers. Why when I wuz yer age, we'd slip off into the woods every now and agin. My granddaddy would have me drag up some dried oak limbs and twigs. We'd root around 'til we found a little lighterd knot or a downed pine that was nearly lighterd. He's splinter off a bit of lighterd and set fire to it under the twigs and such. We never made coffee fires with lighterd—it smoked a lot. You kin start a fire even in the rain with lighterd! You jus' have to git it good 'n hot—so's it'll catch. You know it's made of condensed pine tree sap. That's why it's so hard. Yankees call it "heart of pine." Shoot! Ther's ol' houses up north that have better'n twenty-inch boards made of tha hearts of big pines. Can you imagine a pine tree that big? Sometimes, he used a dry cabbage palm fan to git things started. Trouble with them wuz they burned hot and fast—but you could get some little stuff started, then we'd add some big wood.

Now I don't know how it all got started. I know my great grand daddy said they made coffee from roasted acorns sometimes. It weren't good but it wuz close to the reel thing. He said it were bettern' nuthin'—but jus' barely. He told my granddaddy that they used chicory in coffee to make it stretch when things got tite in the war. I knew a Navy man once that always put eggshells and salt in his coffee—I never knew why. Anyways, the way we make it is simple. After you git yer fire goin'—burnin' down to some coals, the first thing you need then is water. Now I've used pond water, creek water, river water, hand-pump water, cow trough water, well pump water, sulfer water, and rain water. Shoot-tee, I've made coffee with pump-primin' water. You know whut I'm talkin about? The ol' hand cranked water pump like we have at the camp house needs to be primed. Whut happens is that the sucker warshers get dry. If you ever git the chanst, look how the thing works. The leather warshers help the piston pull water up to the pump while you crank the handle. Ther's always a little water left to pour in the top of the pump to wet the leathers sos you can get the pump primed. Oncst the leather soak up the water some, they grab the sides of the walls of the pump and form suction that moves the water up and out. Anyways you'll have to see one to unnerstand whut I'm talkin about. I used the jug of the primin' water to make coffee oncst. It was a little rusty, but I got 'er down.

I usually rinse out the pot since spiders and such'll nest in 'em if you ain't used them in a while. Why, one time I found baby mice in a pot. I put them in the wood pile.

So you start the water to boilin'. I set the pot off to the edge of the big fires or on a small bed of coals to the side. Oncst the water is in a rollin' boil, I pour in a generous amount of coffee grounds. It'll foam up and run over if you don't watch. I set the pot aside to keep it hot but not boilin. I stir it with a clean stick an' let 'er sit a while. After a bit, I stir it agin and add some cool water—this settles the grounds a bit. Then I don't stir it anymore—it ready to drink then. So pour yerself a cup and set back to drink it and watch the fire. Don't git in too big a hurry—it's hotter'n blue blazes at first. Be gentle to not stir up the settled grounds in yer cup. I always drink it through my teeth to keep the grounds out my mouth.

I remember one time goin' to the Collier house in Wauchula. Miz Collier, Wayne's mama, lived ther' on the ol' homestead place. She had her son's dogs that stayed there with her. They wuz mean dogs. You had to call out to her so's she could come to the door. The dogs laid under the porch—they'd come out after you like yellow jackets if'n you stepped out without her there. Anyways she'd holler, "Leave 'im alone boys! Come on in." Miz Collier wuz a friendly lady. She'd always ask if you had time for coffee. That day I had her put on a pot. Her son Wayne wuz ther', too. So she made coffee. I heard that she'd look at you funny if'n you asked for sugar or milk. I took it straight up like a man. It were the rankest stuff I ever tasted. She noticed it wuz a little strong. So she kept stirrin' it like that would help it some. It jus' got ranker. Wayne cocked his eyes at me as if to say, "That's Mama." I never let on.

She poured the coffee from our cups back through the grounds and kept pourin' and stirrin'. I guess she thought that pouring it back into the grounds would lighten it up some—but it just kept getting bitter. It got ranker and ranker. She kept addin' a little to our big mugs after we took a drink— worse'n a danged café waitress in town. Wellsir, she got up and left the table for somethin' and Wayne grabbed both our mugs and poured them in the sink. He turned back to the table and filled our cups agin. Then Mama come back to the table. She picked up the pot and noticed it wuz near empty. She said, "Y'all want me to build another pot?" We said in unison, "Naw, it sure wuz good, Mama." She seemed plum satisfied.

Wayne said, "We got to go to the barn, Mama." I told her, "Thanks a lot Miz Collier—I sure enjoyed yer coffee … ."

When we wuz safely a ways from the house Wayne said, "Son! Mama sure makes rank coffee. I believe it would unloosen rusty bolts."

"It mite make a good paint remover," I said. We smiled and went on to workin' the calves. I remember her well. I sure do miss her. She liked the way I drank her coffee, always delighted when I ast her to build a pot. I think that's where the term,"build a pot of coffee", came from in my mind. She truly "built a pot". One cup of it would last for the whole day.

I heard once that Wayne set down his cup of Mama's coffee on the back porch. He wuz workin' on a saddle or somethin'. He said that a big mosquito flew in and lit on the edge of the cup. Well, this ol' mosquito bogged his bill down into that coffee and loaded up a snout full. Wayne said he watched him start shakin' and havin' a little fit of some kind. He said that mosquito tried to fly off and crashed into an oak tree, bendin' it over some. He said that mosquito couldn't git off the ground good. He kept flyin' around in big circles, crashing into fences, bushes and the ol' horse barn. It spooked the horses, the calves and chickens and almost wrecked the whole place. Wayne said he came back the next mornin', lookin' for another cup. I don't know if he wuz pullin' my leg. Whut do you think?

Wayne said for a time he used to take her coffee out on the back porch with him. When she wasn't looking he'd toss it on a little guava tree there beside the porch. He said that tree got to acting funny—it'd shake and tremble when he came out in the mornings. He said the tree eventually shook so hard that the some of the leaves began to fall off. The fruit got plum black in color and was as bitter as quinine. It took nearly a year for it to settle down after he quit tossin the coffee on it, although it never produced any seedlings after that. I always thought if Wayne were to ever git sick in the hospital, I'd take him some of Mama's coffee. Maybe just the threat of it would get him going … .

My granddaddy told me about a fella on the first railroad down in the Everglades. He said that they didn't know how to build the tracks when they first went into that country. It seems that some farmers got the idea to put in big gardens down there. It wuz rich soil, too. The first year they'd have bumper crops. The second year, everythin' would be ate up by insects. They soon found that you couldn't plant the same plot every year. Wellsir, the railroad went through some of the glades. It wuz quite a ride. The tracks were laid durin' the dry season when the muck wuz fairly hard. The rains came and the muck got plum rubbery soft. They said the trains rolled as it went through the country, like a big ship on soft rollin' waves. Up and down it'd go. Women laughed and the kids squealed in delight. He said that there wuz this one fella on the train that wadn't from around here. Granddaddy said he wuz wearin' knee-high lace-up boots, a flannel shirt and carried a walkin' stick. That wuz a dead giveaway that he wuz from sommers else.

Anyways, the fella had a steel jug of some kind. My granddaddy called it a "Ther'-moose Jug." I don't know exactly whut it wuz, but he said the man poured hisself a cup of coffee into the lid of the thing. As the train gently rolled up and down on the waves of soft muck, the fella juggled the cup so's it wouldn't spill. Granddaddy said he watched him for the longest time, but the man never spilled a drop ... .

One time Granddaddy wuz goin' on a huntin' trip up near Steinhatchee. He said there wuz a one-lane bridge near there that only one vehicle could cross at a time. One day he wuz halfway across it when a car loads of Yankee tourists pulled on it. He wuz in a Model T, they wuz in a ugly green Kaiser. So they jus' up and stopped about a third the way across the bridge and started blowin' ther' horn and hollerin' out the windows. He said they had a plum funny way of talkin'. "Hey Cracker, youse need to back up and let us by," they shouted. He sat there, sayin' nuthin'. On and on they went. The commenced to fog out of their vehicle and gathered up in front of his. Now he wuz more than half way across, so's he figured he had the right-away.

It didn't seem so to them. He never said a word. He jus' got out and rummaged around in his huntin' gear, pullin' out a coffee pot. He walked back on the bridge and down to the water's edge, drawing a pot of water. He looked around for wood. The Yankees jus' watched in shear amazement. Whut wuz this Cracker doin'? they thought.

Finally, one of them asked him, "What are you doing? Don't you see we have to cross this bridge?"

He smiled and said, "It looks like we're gonna be here a while, so I makin' coffee."

They wuz plum stunned. They stared back and forth at each other until finally one said, "Alright, alright, we'll back up." They loaded up and backed off the bridge.

He poured out the water, tossed the pot in the back and then drove off. He smiled a sweet smile at them as he drove away.

Granddaddy said he wuz in the deep woods once on a bird huntin' trip. He and a buddy had made camp near a pond and they wuz all ready for bed about midnight. Now I don't know if you know yet how dark it can be in the woods, but, buddy, it's Dark.

Right abou then, they heard some vehicles comin' ther' way. They stopped a ways off and changed direction straight for their camp.

Two vehicles pulled up right on the edge of camp, shinin' their light right into it. Granddaddy and his buddy crawled away from the firelight. He went into the dark under the Model T and his buddy went into a palmetto patch. Wellsir, the vehicles jus' set there with their lights shinin' on the camp. Granddaddy eased over and slipped the coffee pot under the Model T with him. He poured hisself a cup, figurin' it would be a long standoff. Whut wuz these gents up to?

After a time and several sips of coffee, he'd had enough of this game. He stepped things up a notch.

He eased his shotgun under the vehicle with him. He eased back the slide and dropped a shell in the chamber, then pushed the button, allowing the slide to slam shut, loadin' a shell in the barrel. "Ka-Lack", it echoed in the dark.

Wellsir, there erupted all kind of pandemonium. People went to divin' out the vehicles and scatterin' like quail. One feller hollered, "Hold yer fire—we're sheriff's deputies—hold yer fire!"

Granddaddy called out, "Whut y'all want?"

"We're lookin' for some escaped chain-gang men—we thought y'all wer them!" one shouted.

"Naw, we're bird huntin'. Come on out." He got up and stood near the truck but where he could duck if need be. They eased out. Everybody settled down then. They built a fresh pot of coffee, then spent time drinkin' it and talkin' way into the night. Whut started out as a touches situation turned out a pleasant time for all.

It seems to me that coffee drinkin' is a social affair of sorts. I remember a time when I wuz goin' over to visit with a new neighbor. He wuz from up north sommers. He seemed like a fine fella. I thought I'd go set a spell on his porch and git to know him. I grabbed a little sack I had and filled it with fresh coffee grounds. I took it with me, figurin' that we'd have a cup as we talked. Now I walked up and said "Hidey." He shook hands with me and I give him the coffee. He went in the house and put it in his cupboard. I never saw a drop of coffee. Now that taught me that people think different on the importance of coffee. As time went on though, I got him around to my way of thinkin'. When he comes to my house, I have coffee waitin' for him. He's learnin'.

So you see, we always drink coffee when we can. There ain't nuthin' better for a saddle sore fella or gal—after a hard day. We sure seem to enjoy it. I 'spect it has to do with the open fire and all. There's somethin' 'bout jus' sittin' and listenin' to the frogs while starin' at the fire. When I taste coffee, I always remember how a lone cow calls to her baby in the night. Or how a bull bellers when he's fussin' about somethin'. Ther's jus' somethin' comfortin' to me when I'm havin' a cup and heard a quail call at dusk. It's plum amazin' how far sound travels on cold nights. Truth is, I've often took the dogs on huntin' trips at night, but I really wanted to build a fire and make coffee while they ran the woods. I'd set by the fire, listen to them runnin' and hear all the sounds of the little night creatures. It wuz a good time for us all. Anyways, I know yer a little young to appreciate coffee, but the time will come when you can drink 'er down with the rest of them. I'll teach you how to make it reel soon.

CHAPTER ELEVEN

THE BIG MOSQUITO

My daddy told me that he had a devil of a time once when he was workin' cattle on the north end of the Big Indian Prairie up near and west of Ft. Drum. It was a hot summer day. The bugs were out and about; even the flies seemed to fly slower than usual. Not a blade of grass nor a palmetto fan was moving. There wasn't a hint of a breeze. Ol' Pied was all hot and sweaty. Daddy had roped a rank bull not long before, just after daylight, and his ol' horse was still tuckered out. You could hardly draw a breath the air was so hot! The saddle was still wet from the thunderstorm that hit 'em late afternoon the day before. They were lookin' for strays. Way off you could see thunderheads building over near Ft. Pierce—and it was still early. Plum interestin' how bad hot it can git so early on a June day. He rode among big patches of palmettos quilting the prairie for as far as the eye could see. Some of them were six to seven feet high. They looked like islands in the prairie grasses. Birds, varmints, and such darted in and out. You could see

87

where hogs had rooted around the patches and the armadillos had burrowed under them. In the distance he said he could see hammocks and trees—evidence of a creek or river. You could even see several ponds on the prairie where the rainwater collected here and there.

In those days there were no fences to speak of. The prairie was mostly open range, but there were pines scattered here and there—some of them big pines, too. Ever so often you'd see a dead pine or one that had fallen over. They would eventually turn to lighterd, the sap condensing into pure hard pine-sap—much harder than drugstore taffy candy. More than once he told me that lighterd sure was good fire starter material on rainy nights.

Daddy said his job was to search out any stragglers that had separated from the main herds that ambled around the prairie. Cattle from many herds mingled and roamed all around. There must have been ten or more cow pens scattered here and there. Anyone could use them but it was expected that they'd be left in some working order when they were done. People would gather the herds and take them to the nearest pens, there to sort them by the brands or by earmarks. Everyone seemed to know whose cattle were whose—but to hear him tell it, there were some mix-ups. He said there were herders who could remember which calf went with which mama. They'd study them for hours at times, memorizing who went with who. The calves and cows would find each other if held in a bunch for a time, but there'd be aplenty of bellering and bawling 'til everyone was reunited. Usually the drivers would let them settle down at the pens, even overnight sometimes, to mammy up the calves.

The cattle seemed to naturally go to the south in the winter months and headed north in the summers. The ol' timers said it wuz because of the mosquitoes. They said that in the winters they weren't so bad around the lake and that's why the cattle would graze down futher south. But in the summers, especially when the rains came real regular, they were rank as could be near the lake.

They told all kinds of stories about how the cattle would become restless when tormented by the clouds of the things. Why, they even told of how cattle had been suffocated by mosquitoes in earlier times. I never saw them that bad myself, but some have. The Seminoles were wise to them—they went up near to Ocala in the summers and came back to Okeechobee in the cooler months of the year.

Daddy said it was just another hot and miserable day on the prairie; then, all of a sudden, he heard something coming through the palmettos. He happened to be coming around the edge of a big thick palmetto patch that bordered a big shallow pond. He said that him and Pied were just amblin' along, about half asleep, when this boogery sound came out the patch. The palmetto fans swizzled this way and that—whatever it wuz, wuz comin after him and he thought he'd better hang a spur in Pied's flank to wake him up some, but Pied wuz way ahead of him, breakin' into a jump just before the spur connected and before this thing go to 'em. He allowed it wuz a big hog, a rank bull, a bear, bull gator or mean cow or something big anyways. He said he didn't take time to figure on it much since Pied wuz already boogered about the whole situation. One quick leap to the left and the edge of the palmettos wuz cleared jus' in time for them to see that it was a gigantic mosquito! The thing wuz huge! Its wings had a span over twenty feet! He said the bill on it looked like a long fence post. Daddy's eyes jus' lite up when he told about it.

Pied decided to take matters into his own hands and pulled out for the open—he wuz wide open in about thirty feet. The danged mosquito took to 'um and come right in behind Pied. It was butt over teakettle for several tense moments.

Since Ol' Pied had a hard mornin' workin', he began to slow down some. The mosquito must have been encouraged since he kept comin'! Now Daddy wuz not noted for thinkin' too deep on matters, but he figured he better come up with an idea and I mean quick! He figured that Pied wuz about to give out. He said it came to him like a dream—why not git this critter hung up in the trees?

So off they went to the thickest strand of pines they could see. Pied seemed to trust him—after all it wuz a lot better than what he had in mind, which wuz to buck Daddy off and head for home. The fact is most of the time Pied wuz a lot more thoughtful than Daddy.

Into the pines they went, circlin', dartin', dodgin' and suckin' back here and there, tryin' to confuse an' wear out the mosquito. It was havin' a devil of a time keepin' up. It seemed to not be able to turn real sharp. They'd dart to the left and the mosquito would fly past them, taking a wide turn to git back after them.

Daddy said he even turned his hat and shirt backwards to make the thing think he wuz goin' in the opposite direction, though he later said it didn't seem to work.

Durin' one of the darts, the mosquito misjudged— he plunged his bill into a pine tree. Before he could pull it out, Daddy jumped off Pied, grabbed a lighterd knot and braded the bill over so's he couldn't pull it out. There wuz all kinds of commotion while the thing beat and frammed the dirt, shakin the tree, while tryin' to pull out his stuck beak from the tree trunk. Daddy said he and Pied took a breather, watchin' the thing for a while. Finally they went on back to cow huntin'.

Six months later Daddy said he went back by that pine where the crazy mosquito had stuck his bill. He smiled when he said, "There wuz enough mosquito bones left to build a set of cow pens."

I thought maybe he wuz tellin' a tall tale.

What do you think?

CHAPTER TWELVE

PARTNER'S CAMPING TRIP

Now you know I have told you about my old friend, Partner. He was a true Florida Cracker. He was born in West Florida near the Florida-Georgia state line but somehow by some way or another he settled in South Florida. He was the mildest, meekest man I ever knew, always pleasant and friendly. Everybody that knew him knew that Partner was known to tell a tall tale or two. When the work was done or sometimes when we were resting, he'd get this far-away look in his eyes, kinda like he was travelin' in his mind to some far-off distant place. He'd remove his straw hat, wipe his white head with a handkerchief and usually start one of these tales with a question.

I recall one day in particular. We were working in a grove, hoeing rank grass from around the little orange trees. It was hotter'n blue blazes—even the birds found shade. Partner said that it was so hot the toads would get in the fire to get in the shade of a skillet. Well sir, up come this toad stranglin' thunderstorm. It built up near us and we had to race to the little barn nearby. The wind twisted the trees; rain came in heavy sheets, the thunder roared at us as we sat in the middle of the shed on a big pile of feed sacks. After a bit, the storm let up a little, settling into a steady rain—we knew that we'd be there a while.

Partner got that look that I mentioned in his eyes. He studied in his mind something—for a long time it seemed. We knew what was comin' and, sure enough, he started with a question. "Have I ever told y'all bout the time I went camping in the Blue Cypress Swamp?" he began. Now even if I'd heard about it I'da said, "No—I never heard that one." Somehow even the retellin' of his stories were real treats to me. Then he began.

"Me and the boys decided to go deer huntin' in the Blue Cypress one time. It was real early in the season. The weather was a little unpredictable and still a little too warm to hunt but we went anyway. I never liked to hunt when it was hot. Y'all know how we have those little hot spells that seem to come here ever' December? That happened to us when we got down there and set up our camp. We got there just as a hot spell started. The air was still, not a leaf stirred in the woods. We built a fire, put on some coffee water and proceeded to set up the big tent. I never owned a tent myself, but one of the fellas had one his uncle gave him. We figured it would be plum nice to sleep in the thing since the mosquitoes were in full bloom at the onset of the warm weather.

"We set 'er up and moved our plunder in it, each man putting his warbag of personals and sleeping gear in piles. Somehow we could get all six of us in there and had a little room to spare. The center pole that held the thing up was stout. Someone tapped a nail into it and hung his jacket on it. It only took an hour to get moved in. We went outside, made a pot of coffee, and collected some more wood for the fire. Dark came on us as we drank coffee, listened to the woods and talked about the plans for the next mornin's hunt.

"Them swamp mosquitoes began to come out—now I mean they come at us full force! We wuz swattin' and flappin' at 'em, tryin' to keep them out'n our noses and so forth. It got plum unbearable. One real smart man said he thought we ought to git in the tent and seal 'er off so we could git out the tormentin' things. That seemed to set well with us all, so we went into the tent and closed the flap. It wadn't too bad inside—a little warm but at least we wuz out the bloodsuckers. We all set up out sleepin' gear and went to bed early—there wadn't anything else to do.

"Man, were those mosquitoes bad! You could hear them whinnin' and zoo-zooin' around the tent—it sounded like a little high-pitched motor runnin' outside. But we were out of them and that wuz all that counted to us. I remember wakin' up in the night some, hearin' them searchin' for a way to get in the tent. I began to wake up real regular like—seemed to me time to git up. It was still plum black outside. I figured that daylight would drive most of the away. That wuz a long night it seemed to me at the time.

"I just lay there thinkin', 'Son! This is sure a long night!' I noticed some of the others wer awake and a bit restless, too. The mosquitoes were still working and it wuz pitch black outside. One fella got up and started shavin' his face under the light of a flashlight. Finally we were all awake. Someone lite a Coleman Lantern so we had plenty of light in the tent. All of us were up, dressin' and puttin' our sleepin' gear in bags. One fella decided to clean his shotgun. You could smell the sweet gun oil. I got everythin' ready. All I wuz waitin' on wuz some hint of daylight so I could build up the fire and put on some water for coffee. 'Breakfast sure will be good today—I'm starvin', I thought. It wuz still pitch dark in the tent and the mosquitoes wer still workin'.

"Well sir, the fella that wuz cleanin' his shotgun forgot that he had a live shell in the chamber. He wuz cleanin' away when he accidently pulled the trigger, blastin' a hole through the top of the tent—it scared the livin' daylights out of us. We wuz stunned to see pure daylight shinin' through—it wuz nearly noon! We went outside and found that the mosquitoes were ten inches thick all over the tent! That shotgun blast had blowed a hole in them a foot wide! We'd been in the pitch black tent for mite near eighteen hours!"

Another tall tale? Mebbe so … .

CHAPTER THIRTEEN

CROW HUNTING

I once wuz on an Elk hunt in Montana. It was colder than all git out. It was so windy and cold that we had to chip the ice off your coffee cups in the mornings. It got so nasty that we had to lay up in the cabin a day or two 'til the weather cleared some. We'd tell stories, drink coffee, sit and sleep by the roaring fire and watch the snow fall. I remember reading a story then. It was in an old Field and Stream Magazine. I can't remember the man's name what wrote it but he wuz really funny to me. I believe his name wuz Ed Zern, but it's been nearly thirty-odd years ago. He told of the fine art of crow hunting. I loved his story and thought you'd like to hear my recollection of it.

Now it seems according to him crows are very, very smart. They can do a lot of damage to a grain crop. Hundreds often show up and peck away at the plants. When they see a hunter, they all take off, flyin' around—all safe and sound in the air. They talk back and forth in squawks and caws. He seemed to think they were communicatin' and allowed as they had the ability to count and keep up with who came to the huntin' field.

In the story he described the building of blinds. These little huts were made so's a fella could git in and peek out at the flyin' crows as they circled the field. A hunter could ease his shotgun out of little openings and shoot at the crows. The huts were built around cornfields or fields of some other grain crop where crows went to belly-up on the grain or seeds. He kept sayin' that his plan wuz a good way to approach huntin' them since crows are highly intelligent and able to count hunters. So according to him they could tell who wuz there, how many hunters there wuz, who wuz where in the blinds and such as that. From the way he told it, the crows could recognize individual hunters. So he come up with a plan for successful crow huntin'.

I cain't rightly remember all he said but here goes. He told as how the first thing to do wuz locate a place where the crows congregated near some big grain field. He allowed as all hunters should gather up in a tight wad at their vehicles and divide up into three groups. Course, the more hunters there were, the better the plan worked. He recommended a high number—oh, say thirty hunters in all. I cain't remember the numbers he used for the number of hunters, so I'll just tone it down for you. Since you're almost eight years old, I'll use seven hunters so you can keep up with the story.

After all seven hunters gather at the grain field, they are to put on hats—all hats are different in style and color. They also will have seven football jerseys with big numbers on them from 1 to 7, but with no number 3 and two number 5's. When everyone's set, three hunters run to the first blind while four run to the middle of the field, two break off, heading to the second blind while two run back to the trucks where everyone had parked. There the two hunters put on numbered football jerseys and stuff all the extra jerseys and the two numbered 5 under their shirts and ran back to the first blind while one from that blind runs for the second blind. On the way, one hunter slips them the two number 5 jerseys to put on when they git to the blind. They are to hand out the extra jerseys to those in the blind. Ever' one but one hunter is now wearin' a jersey.

When a little time has passed, two hunters from the second blind run for the parkin' area and git under their trucks and change jerseys and hats. As they are gettin' close to the trucks, three hunters run to the second blind—one of them wearin' number 2 and another wearin' number 7. Now when they git there, the two hunters from under the truck must come out wearin' different hats and numbers and run to the first blind, one of them changing jerseys to number 4 and then running back to the second blind.

At this point I git plum befuzzled when I think about it. I figure if I cain't keep up with all the numbers in the blinds, the crow certainly couldn't. But it gits worse.

In a few minutes, four hunters from the second blind must run to meet two from the first blind, then gather in the middle of the field, change hats and the jerseys numbered 4, 2, 6, 7, 1 and 5 and should also switch shotguns. Then the hunters with jerseys number 4 and 7 turn their jerseys inside out so the crows can't see the numbers. They run back to the trucks and get into two trucks and drive them about thirty yards, leavin' the motors runnin'. While they are movin' the trucks, number 6, 2, 7 and 1 hunters run to the first blind, switch caps, jerseys, and put on fake beards and mustaches, then they run back to the trucks.

How many hunters are left in the blinds? After all this runnin' and switchin' this leaves one single solitary hunter left in the second blind. If they have done it right, the crows ought to be as confused as a termite in a yo-yo. The fella that wrote the story said that there ought to be an ambulance there in case somebody gits sick from all the runnin'. As I recall he also said that sometimes the crows are so smart that it takes some alterin' of speed and runnin' at odd angles to cause the crows to have to use geometry and trigonometry to keep up.

See, the idea wuz to confuse the crows. Now I don't remember all the exact numbers so, like I say, I made up my own. I never tried anything such as this method. It seems an awful lot of work to git one hunter where he can shoot at a crow. But then agin, I've seen crows do some perty smart things. It wouldn't surprise me if they could count good.

Anyway, we all had a laugh at the story on a cold morning in Montana.

CHAPTER FOURTEEN

TINY CINDY RELLA

My grandmamma tole me this story one time in front of tha' fireplace one cold winter night. She said the cold creepin' under the door reminded her of a story about the Bad Luck Rella Family. We wuz visitin' her at Ft. Drum at the time. It sounded kinda familiar to me but I did'n dare tell Granny I'd already heard it told different. She rocked before the fire, puffed her corn-cob pipe and told us all about 'em. This is tha' way she told it.

Now at the place called Ol' Camp Starvation, which ain't too far frum here, by tha way, lived the Rella family. The closest settlement to them wuz Opal, a small turpentine camp of about fifteen shacks. Wher' the Rella folks come from nobody knows, but I heard talk that they come from Calhoun, Georgia where their great-grand-daddy settled after the War Between the States. Somehow or another tha family moved to these parts in the late 1800s. It's said that tragedy seemed to foller them ever' wher' they went. They come here with only their belongin's and a milk

103

cow on a string. The Rellas were reely hard workers. They built them a cabin, a barn and some cow pens. That old milk cow they had wuz a goodun—she had a calf every year. They planted some orange trees and traded at the settlement at Opal. After a time they ended up with a small herd of cattle. They lived off the land as wuz a mite easier then than nowadays.

After settling in, it wasn't long before there was a brand new, right-out-of-the-poke baby girl born there on the Rella farm in the oak hammock. They named her Cindy, after Old Man Rella's first cousin's mother-in-law's sister's second child's daughter's best friend. Her name wuz Cindy Appen de Sidus. So the family grew and grew. The next year Mama Rella had a big ol' boy. They named him Cletus, after Mama Rella's fifth-born sister's third boy, who never amounted to much, I'm told. Things were going good at the Ol' Camp Starvation home place. Two Yankee surveyors named it that when they run out of whisky.

As Cindy grew, it were plain to see that she wuz a beauty of a child. She wuz tiny! I mean tiny like her mother! But she wuz purtier than a speckled birddog puppy. When she had growed up to some eighteen years old, tragedy struck the Rella family agin.

Now the Rellas were smart, even if they had a black cloud over their family. They built the old cabin like the rest of the Crackers there. It wuz simple but a good home for tha' four of them. The home wuz whut they call a "dog-trot style". That means there was an open hallway right down the center of it, with two big rooms on each side of the hall. The tin roof covered tha' whole thing and ther' wuz a fireplace at one end. The hall let air move through tha house reel good. One of tha' big rooms wuz divided to make little bedrooms in them. The other room wuz a big room with a dinner table, the fireplace and some chairs. The kitchen wuz outside in a little shack. A roof covered the way to the house. That' a-ways if the kitchen caught fire, the house would mostly be safe. They thought so anyways … . After livin' in the house for nigh on to twenty years, the wood wuz really dry. That's where the bad luck reared its ugly head agin.

One cold Jan'ary night, Cindy and her little brother, Cletus were firing the grove. That means they wuz keeping little fires going under their orange trees tryin' to keep the new crop of oranges frum freezin'. It wuz their turn to keep the fires goin'. Their Paw and Mama would spell them after midnight until daylight when it gets the coldest durin' a freeze in Florida.

They had on all the clothes they had, tryin' to keep warm, don't ya know. They'd pile a few lighterd knots on one fire then another and sit by one to keep warm. That's when the tragedy struck—the cabin caught fire and killed their mama and daddy and their littlest brother, Roy. Cindy saw the cabin fire by the orange glow reflectin' off the cabbage palms near the house. She and Cletus ran to it in time to see the main timbers fall in and the whole thing caved in. Mama, Daddy and Little Roy were gone.

They cried and cried. At daylite Cindy thought it best to go to the Evans Place, about six miles away as the dog trots.

Arrivin' there at breakfast time for the Evans', they told the story of the fire and the lost Rella family. Mr. Evans wuz real considerate and understandin'. He told them to move in with the Evans family. This didn't suit Miz Beulah Evans—she jus showed her country behind... she'd have none of it. She said, "Horace, this ain't gonna work. There's too much work here now and we already got two girls. Neither one is married yet." But Mr. Horace Evans was Cap. (That means he wuz captain and his word stood over all the fuss.) The command made Miz Evans madder'n a cornered bobcat. She fussed and fumed around all mornin', slammin' things here and ther'. Mr. Evans decided it wuz time for a cow huntin' trip to the woods. He knew it'd take a while before Miz Evans settled down. He packed a tote sac full of grits, fatback bacon, coffee, venison jerky and whutever else he needed, saddled his horse and one fer Cletus an' they pulled out.

Tha' Evans girls were a little on the homely side of things. Tha' thing is, they wuz ugly—not so much on the outside but on the inside, though they both had big feet. If nuthin' else this is whut made them tough customers. The locals called them, "Tha' Big-footed Evans Girls." The oldest, Ima, wuz the biggest. Eura wuz sneaky and spent most of her time followin' Ima, both lookin' for trouble an' eventually some way to make Cindy Rella's life tough. Now whut wuz funny, when the Evans girls weren't around, the other kids called them, "Ima Big-footed Evans" and "Eura Big-footed Evans." The girls would knock a knot on yer head if'n they heard it said. They jus' bout hated every body around.

The days went on, Cindy's life changed for the worse. She ended up doin' all or most all the chores, while her new step-sisters, Ima and Eura sat on the front porch and lolled away the hours. Cindy did all the laundry, the ironin', the gardenin' and cookin' and fed the horses and pigs. Mama Evans wuz meaner than a stomped-on snake. She jawed at Cindy all tha' time. Do this and that and when yer through find something else to do wuz her approach to bein' a step-mother. Time seemed to drag on and on for poor tired Cindy Rella.

One day a neighbor stopped at the house and asked if the Evans' had heard the news. He went on about the big buckout social that wuz set for Sat'day after next—over at the Whiddon Place. (Y'all mite not know a buckout is whut some crackers call a party or a dance.) Mr. Whiddon had just got the contract to dredge a canal out of Lake Okeechobee all the way to Ft. Myers and he wanted to celebrate his good fortune. Mr. Whiddon's son, Junior, wuz also gonna work as the oiler and lanchman on the dredge. Mr. Whiddon wuz rollin' in the dough and he wanted Junior to settle down and git married. He figured a new bride might just keep him on the job. So, the truth is, word had already spread to all the gals in the whole of tha' woods. Ther' wuz a heap of gals interested in ol' Junior. He wuz plum handsome. He had all his teeth and hair, didn' chew or drink (much anyways) and took a bath every Friday night. Junior would be a good catch. Anyways it seems that the whole country around and abouts wuz invited. People wuz to bring some food or bread and come to dance allnite.

Miz Evans saw an opportunity to marry off one of the gals at least and maybe two. Ima and Eura wuz real excited. Cindy didn't know much about Junior or the Whiddon Family. All she'd heard wuz they was prominent people in Okeechobee County. The mean step-sisters made Cindy Rella make their dresses. Miz Evans had been savin' material from the flour sacks when she'd used up all the flour. The material would make fine print dresses for the girls. Course, they were going to be real long since the girls were touchus about their big feet. So Cindy made them fine dresses on an old foot-cranked sewing machine that come from Sears. Now there wuz just enough material left for Cindy Rella to make her a dress, too, but try as she mite, she couldn' hide her purty figure— ther' weren't enough flour sacks to make it big and loose. Ima and Eura thought all the time that she wuz workin on their dresses only. Ima tried hers on. It wuz a little tite. It popped like a can of store bought biscuits opening when she unbuttoned it. Even Eura and Mama laughed when it happened. Eura said, "I swear,

Ima, I'm gonna change your name to 'Biscuit'." With that she ran off for a few hours to let Ima cool down.

The day for the buckout came and the dressed-up Evans women pulled out for the Whiddon Place about noon. They carried some fried chickens, a fresh-cut cabbage heart, a big pan of lima beans with ham hock in 'em and a couple of pies and a cobbler. Ol' Lady Belle pulled the wagon away at a slow pace. Laughin' and gigglin' out over the scrub the Evans women went.

It wadn't long before Cindy Rella heard a noise in the barn. One of the pigs squealed, a frightened chicken run out tha barn and one of the puppies barked. She wuz a little afraid. But it wuz Mr. Evans. He came out with the gentle old mare named, Lulu. She wuz saddled up with a side saddle, made for women-folk. He'd borried it from the neighbors.

"I do declare!" said Cindy. "Whut chew doin' here, Mr. Evans? Where's Cletus?"

"Me and Cletus are re-buildin' yer old cabin that burnt up. He's gonna stay ther'." Then his face spread out in a big wide grin and he said, "I seen the wife and girls leave and figured it wuz safe for me to come in. I cain't take all the fussin' at times. I heard about the buckout and thought I'd see if you wanted to go. You go on and git ready, I got some things to do in the barn. Whutever you do, be back here before Beulah and the girls git home and keep out of their site at the party."

"Why, Mr. Evans, that's plum nice of ya to think of me. I'd luv to go" said a smiling Cindy Rella.

She ran into the house and took a bath, combed her hair, put on her new dress, and pinched her cheeks in front of the mirror to make them blushed. She hesitated; she didn't have no shoes! She thought, "I cain't go all dressed up an no shoes." Sad and all teary-eyed, she went to the porch to call Mr. Evans and tell him she couldn't go. As she opened the door, there on the door step wuz the prettiest pair of new boots she'd ever seen. She looked out at the barn. Mr. Evans wuz sittin' out front of it on a tree stump, whittlin'. When he saw her, he started grinnin' like a mule eatin' sawgrass.

"'Spect you'll need them," he said. She ran to him and threw her arms around him, embarrassing him as she did it.

"You're the best step-daddy any girl could have. Thank you kindly," said Cindy.

He grinned and kicked the dirt a little, then said, "Yer the best step-gal any man could have. You make me smile ever time I see ya. Now, you git... Cut across the hammock and you'll be ther' in no time. Lulu knows the way home."

Off Lulu went in a gentle lope. Across the hammock, through the woods, across Taylor's Creek at the crossin' place and south to the Whiddon Place they rode. On the north side of the Whiddon Place, in the piney flatwoods, she first heard the fiddle music. It sounded good. She heard the fiddlin' of some ol' tunes as she rode, tunes like Paddy's Leather Breeches, The Skye Boat Song, Miss MacLeod of Raasay and The Rose Among the Heather.

110

After tying ol' Lulu to a myrtle bush, she slipped in reel quiet like. Next thing you know she wuz asked to dance and dance she did! Round and round she danced with different fellas that kept cuttin' in. Fact is, she wuz a natural dancer and she wuz reel purty. On top of that she wuz the pertiest one of the bunch, so's it ain't no wonder that a fight broke out amongst the eligible bachelors of the lot. Junior stood off to the side, enjoyin' the best buckout he'd ever been to. Where can ya go and see all yer neighbors, hear good fiddlin', watch a good headskinnin' in progress and eat such fine groceries?

Then his smilin' eyes fell on Cindy Rella. Son—I want to tell ya, it wuz all over at the point... he was hooked like a catfish on a dough ball!

Whilst the fight continued, he asked Cindy Rella to dance, 'cause the fiddler had cranked up agin. So on the edge of a dust cloud of swingin' elbows, knees and fists and a little behind the crowd of on-lookers, they danced as if they wuz the only ones in the world. One fella wuz tossed over the heads of the crowd by Baby O'Steen. Baby wuz tougher than the bark on a oak tree. Ol' Junior had to break it up a bit—things wuz getting' out of hand... So into the fray he went, knockin' this and that one as he come to 'em. Him an' Baby got back to back and took on the whole grinnin' bunch. When the dust cleared, Baby wuz slappin' Junior on his back and Junior wuz wipin' the dust off'n his new store bought shirt. The rest of the fellas wuz laying out or propped up with people fannin' them. Most agreed that this wuz the best buckout they'd ever been to. The fiddler kept playin' and the people kept laughin'.

Then Junior looked back to where he'd left Cindy Rella, but she figured she better git back home before the Evans' seen her. She had slipped off in such a hurry, with Junior behind her callin' her name, she hung one of her new boots in a palmetto root and it wuz jerked plum off her foot. The root sprung back and tossed the boot behind her. It wuz dark by now, there wuzn't time to go back for it so she skedaddled on to Lulu and rode home at a fast pace.

The next few days wuz settled down to normal, but Junior wuz sicker than a horse colt that ate 50 pounds of chicken feed. He wuz plum heart sick. All he had to show fer his search wuz a new tiny boot. Mr. Whiddon saw that his boy wuz thunderstruck by the new gal that nobody seemed to know. He told Junior, "Boy, take that boot and go by all the neighbors to see if you can find the gal that lost it." Junior pondered this for a day then decided that he'd do just that. So he saddled Ol' Buck and made out to make the circuit of all the neighbors.

After three days of searchin' without any prospects, he purty much had whut he would say down pat. He said, "I danced with a purty gal at the buckout last Sat'day, I couldn't git a good look at her but I know she wuz the purtiest gal I ever saw. She wuz as polite as a princess. She wuz a tiny thing and she laughed a lot as we danced. She left her new boot behind before I got her name and I aim to find her. Will all the gals here try it on so's I can find the love of my heart?" This astounded the men folk, caused the mamas to cry and the gigglin' gals to line up for a try-on.

He arrived at the Evans Place about dusk on the third day. They knew him and had already heard he wuz prowlin' about, lookin' for his lost princess. Upon hearin' his quest, Ima and Eura lined up to try for the fittin' of the boot. They sat on the porch step as he placed the boot on the ground before them. When he saw Ima's big foot going for the boot he said, Whoa!" Ima paused but went on workin' at gettin' the boot on. Her big foot wouldn' even go into the boot top, much less into the foot of it. In frustration, Ima pouted as she threw the boot to Eura. Same thing happened to Eura, only this time when he saw her foot he said, "Son!" (He'd heard about the Big-footed Evans gals but this way more than he expected. Realizin' they wuz touchus about them, he let it drop.)

Disappointed again, he asked, "Miz Evans is that all of yer girls?" "Yes it is" she replied. So Junior headed for his horse and prepared to mount when Mr. Evans steps out the barn, sayin', "Hey Junior... No, that ain't all the girls here; we got one more, my step-daughter Cindy Rella. Beulah go git Cindy." He said it in such a stern voice that Miz Evans shivered a little. Not only wuz she surprised as his showin' up all of a sudden, she knew he meant bidness. He wuz a good man but he could git riled. He could only take so much contention before he got that way—but she knew he'd reached his limits. When they had first married, she crossed him once and he ripped her dress off. She never crossed him again when he gave her the same "look" he did that day—and that wuz thirty years ago! She quickly ran to the back of the house where Cindy Rella wuz sewin' on Ima's new dress with a busted bodice from her breathin' in reel deep before sneezin'. (It sounded like a 410 shotgun when it busted!)

"Come quick, Cindy. Horace is fit to be tied. Git out ther' and do whut he says" Miz Evans said. Cindy put down her sewin' and headed to the porch. She wuz plum speechless when she saw Junior standin' there on the stoop. By this time it were reel dark, so's he couldn't recognize her.

Mr. Evans said, "Cindy, this here is Junior Whiddon. He's lookin' for a gal he saw and danced with at the buckout. She lost her boot. Try it on and he'll know if'n it wuz you or not." He winked at her after he said it. Cindy's heart wuz fluttering like a covey of quail leaving a gopher hole. She sat down on the porch step and slipped the boot on with ease. About that time, Miz Evans walks out with a coal oil lantern and Junior could finally see Cindy's face. Astonished, he said, "It's you! I've found you at last!" He held his arms wide as Cindy ran to him and gave him a big hug." She then ran over and hugged a red-faced Mr. Evans and said, "Thanks, Daddy."

Junior asked Cindy Rella if she would marry him and she smiled and said, "Whut kept you so long... Yes."

Mr. Evans brought ol' Lulu out, saddled and ready to go. He said to Junior, "When you git home, turn ol' Lulu loose, she'll come home."

Things improved a consider amount as Cindy mounted Lulu. She wuz a reel princess and Junior wuz to be a king in this backwoods country. The Evans' all waved goodbyes. Then Ima sneezed again and busted her old dress just like the new one that Cindy Rella just fixed.

Eura called her "Biscuit" and ran for the barn with Ima on her heels. Mr. Evans grinned at Beulah and she grinned back. Maybe things would be tolerable now.

CHAPTER FIFTEEN

MAMA AND THE DOCTOR

Did I ever tell you 'bout tha time my mama called
the doctor? She was a fine woman but she wuz headstrong. My brothers and sisters added up to eight in
all. My mama was able to hold us all together some
how—even when times were tough. Why… I remember when she had a baby in the morning and got out
of bed to fix supper that night. She didn't know no
better I expect.

My mama also had a strange way of naming us
kids. She usually named us after someone in the
family or some influential person in the county. For
instance, she named the first child, Lee Roy. (Funny,
he named his boy Roy Lee…) Then there was Clair,
Causey, Carol Lynn, Cullen, Casper, Custer and me,
Lou Lou.

Now ther's ah story behind ever' name. When it
came to namin' my oldest brother, she couldn't make
up her mind. She liked Robert E. Lee, but didn't like
Robert 'cause it reminded her of the fella down the
road a piece that cut down her favorite guava tree.

She thought "E' wuz a little too short and she didn't know how to spell it. On the other hand she liked Roy 'cause Roy Rogers was a fine fella. So she settled on Lee Roy—to her way of thinkin' it were the best of both.

Clair was named after her Uncle Montclair. Mama debated a bit about whether to use, "Mont", "Monty" or "Clair", but since sister wuz a girl she figured Clair would do. One of the neighbor boys said she wuz so ugly she had to sneak up on a glass of water. (I thumped his head 'bout it and he never said it agin.)

Causey wuz named after her first Sunday school teacher, Mr. Billie Bob Causey. He wuz the one who had to apologize to the choir one time in front of the whole congregation. (Seems that when he wuz puttin' tha letters on the sign out in front of the church, he put "Song Festival Tonight!" Then he spelled out whut the preacher asked him to put for the title of his sermon. It wuz a catchy phrase: "If You Want to Know What Hell Is, Come Tonight!" Hell wuz whut Preacher planned to preach on… the problem wuz it wuz right under the choir's sign…)

Carol Lynn was named after Mama's first cousin's sister's husband's mother's sister's best friend. (She was the one who could put a pool ball in her mouth and hum Dixie, but that's 'bout all she could do.) Carol Lynn was so fat we had to grease the door facin's and dangle a sausage biscuit outside to get her through the door way. She had to go to on a trip one time. The bus driver wooden take out the

118

middle arm-rest between tha seats so she couldn't sit. Paw asked if he would clear out a baggage section underneath so we could put her an' a box of ham sandwiches and some RC Colas in ther' with her. The driver didn't go for the idea. So Mama made two shoeboxes full of fried chicken and some apple pies an' we pulled our ol' truck down to the hard road—tha one that didn't have a motor. Paw put a tow rope in the back with Carol Lynn in the cab with a sign that said, "Micanopy." Wellsir, it wadn't no time at all before somebody hooked up and pulled her to Kenansville. Frum ther' somebody pulled her to Ocala. Then she got a tow to Micanopy. She stayed with kinfolks for three weeks, ate them outta house and home an' come back in a truck without a motor and two more shoeboxes of fried chicken. Didden cost us a dime an' we didden use a teaspoonful of gas either...

Cullen was named after Ol' Joe Cullen the fiddle player. He used to play at all the buckouts startin' when Mama wuz just ah toddler. She got her love fer fiddlin' frum tunes like Skye Boat Song, Shady Glade, Miss Ada Crawford and others like them. Ya mite say Mama wuz plumb duncey 'bout fiddle music. We didn't mind when Cullen wadn't partial to fiddle, but it always bothered her that he wadn't. The fact is he never wuz interested in fiddles... tha only thing he wuz good at wuz makin' a sound like a horsefly. When we had trouble getting' tha horses in tha barn, we'd call Cullen. He'd start that buzzin' and the horses would run to tha barn. We used to call him Cullen Horsefly 'til he got a little mean about tha teasin'.

We never knew wher' she come up with Casper for a name ... he was a skinny baby. He wuz so skinny when he grew up he could stand under tha shade of a clothesline and not git wet when it rained. He didn't weigh as much as a wild grapefruit when he wuz born... we always thought she named him Casper after Casper Johnson, the preacher. Both of 'em were kinda loud when they talked. Mama never told us why she named him that. Paw always said she run outta names so's she just used whatever popped into her mind. We did have a man named Truman Kasmer Bernsteen in the family. He married Mama's brother's daughter's daughter who lived in St Louie. Truman owned a tayler's shop and made suits for river boat gamblers. (I think Mama wuz embarrassed 'bout not spellin' it rite, so she never brung it up.)

Mama said Custer wuz named after the General that got whipped out west. She told Paw that he wuz the last stand for her and ther'd be no more. (But I fooled 'em when I showed up.) Custer wuz tough, too. He wuz the one that went on tha hog huntin' trip and killed tha biggest boarhog in the area. We'd just bought a big chest freezer frum Sears & Roebuck an' he put the hog in it to cool.... Well, the hog wern't dead... he come to and tore the insides of that new freezer to smithereens. We called Sears and tole them whut happened. Paw asked if they'd stand behind their freezer and replace it. The man said, "I looked all through the warranty and hit don't say ah thing 'bout hog damage." (It woodena been so bad if Custer hadn't heard the ruckus, opened the lid and let the boarhog out.) Custer and Causey near shot the place apart by the time they kilt it. Made Paw madder'n ah nestful of hornets.

But I wuz the biggest baby on record for tha county at the time—still might be the biggest fer all I know. Mama told us she tried to have me all one day an' most of a nite. Ol' Doc Hill came and sat with her tha whole time. She said he'd slip off ever now and then and have a nip of somethin'… said he'd come back to her side smellin' like sire mash whiskey. Anyways, Mama said I finally arrived real early in the morning. The doctor wuz a little too tipsy to fill out the birth certificate. An', too, Mama wuz plumb exhausted. She tried to remember her great uncle's name but she wuz too tired to walk to the cemetery to read his name off the headstone. (Frum whut they said, I don't reckon tha doctor coulda spelled anything at the time) I laid ther' fer a few days while all the kin and neighbors come by to leave groceries and see whut a fifteen-pound baby looked like. Uncle Eulie, when he saw me, said, "Boy… ain't he a lulu?" Mama said she liked it for a name, so she named me "Lou Lou." The doctor came by to check on Mama in a few days and he filled in the birthin' certificate. (I wuz sure glad she didn't name me after whut my Aunt Josephine said, "I swear Della, he's a belly-buster." (How would that be to be called "Belly Buster" Driggers? I'da had to go by "B.B.")

121

But back to my story. Mama wuz a little set in her ways. She'd line all us kids up twice a year for our caster oil treatment. To her way of thinkin' that whut kept us all healthy and free of worms. We hated it but we knew not to run frum her 'cause when she caught us we'd git a switchin'. Ever spring an' fall she'd get out the caster oil and the big spoon an' we'd line up for our doses. I hated the stuff. I can still taste it today. This wuz the tradition in our home.

One year Carol Lynn ate too many green guavas and wuz sicker'n a colicked horse. She had one bad belly ache. Mama wuz afraid she'd die so she called the new doctor in town. He come out to tha house and looked Carol Lynn over. He give her somethin' to settle her down. He said she'd be fine. Mama never wasted a doctor's visit. She lined us all up and had the doctor look over each one of us. Ever'body had a turn before the doctor. He looked down our gullets, poked and prodded us in the bellies, looked for lice and listened to us breathe. He said we wuz all fine. Mama wanted to get her money's worth so she asked some questions. "Tell me Doctor, whut do you think of me givin' all my youngin's caster oil twice a year to clean them out an' such?" she asked.

The doctor smiled and replied, "Miz Driggers, I don't think it's worth a d - - - (*he said a word my Mama wouldn't let us say so I cain't write it either...*) When us kids heard that we all broke out in plumb wild clapping an' cheerin'—all eight of us! (Even Carol Lynn perked up and clapped when she heard whut he said.) Mama wuz not too impressed with the doctor's views. She turned to us and we quieted down real quick. She paid him three dollars and gave him a hen, a dozen eggs an' some tomatoes.

All I remember now is before the dust cleared from his ol' Model T, she had us lined up—you guessed it—for a dose of caster oil.

CHAPTER SIXTEEN

THE PLOTT HOUNDS AND THE CIRCUS BEAR

When I wuz a young man I'd git notions to do things that sometimes didden work out like I planned. Me and Johnny used to hunt al over the country here 'bouts. Johnny had asthma—you could hear him wheezing when we'd be slippin' up on game. I liked him and he liked me. We spent a lotta time in the woods together. He later became a deputy for the sheriff's office south of here. In them days, Clearwater wuz nothin' but a little ol' town on the gulf coast of Florida, but things picked up in the winter with the tourists and all. Bicyclers would flood in the little hotels and they'd race her' an' ther', wearin' funny lookin' outfits, too. Why, even the circus wintered not far from there. In the spring the circus would start the trip up north and Clearwater wuz often one of their stops—but I git ahead of myself.

Friday afternoons Johnny would show up with his shotgun, a coffee pot, some white rice, a Dutch oven and a tarpaulin; I'd git my shotgun, some shells an' ah couple of blankets an' we'd load up my ol' coupe an' pull out for the woods. I had an ol' car that served well as a huntin' buggy. We had skinny tires on it. It had a big trunk we could carry a dog or two when we wanted to deer hunt. If we come to deep water, Johnny'd lay the tarp over the front of it an' we'd plow through it—but we didn't dare stop 'cause the water'd git in the engine. We usually camped in a hammock, near ah creek or pond so we'd have fresh water for cookin'. While one of us set up camp, the other'd go shoot a few squirrels to make perlue. (That's slow-stewed rice an' squirrel.)

On one of these trips we got to talkin' near-about everything. I told Johnny 'bout tha dogs I'd seen in Ocala. They were frum North Carolina. A man named Plott up there summers bred bear dogs. Supposedly, these dogs would track a bear an' circle 'um while they took turns nippin' the bear in tha' butt. The ol' bear would whirl around to catch the dog that nipped him an' another'n would nip him. (Sounded to me like they just worried 'em 'til the hunter's caught up with 'um. It was claimed they had good noses and would hunt anythin'. Ther' wuz lots of bear in tha' woods in them days, but they didn't bother us and we didn't them.)

The Plott Hounds I saw in Ocala were big ol' dogs. They looked like Black and Tans or Redbone Hounds but the colors wuz different. The ones I saw were big-boned, droopy-eared and speckled hounds. They could be red-, brown- or blue-brindled or near 'bout solid in color. They looked a lot like a Blood Hound but were more compact an' didn't have so much ear and wrinkles. I thought we ought to get a couple and see whut they could do in Florida.

So we borrowed a phone an' called my friend in Ocala. He give us the address of Mr. Plott. I wrote him, askin' if he had a couple of his hounds for sale. We finally worked a deal and I bought two fine ones. He told me they were still young—jus' big ol' ganglin' puppies, but they'd started goin' with the grown dogs on hunts. He said, "They'll do—they ortta be crackerjack dogs." He put them in a crate and sent 'em down to Wildwood on the train. Me an' Johnny drove up an' paid the delivery bill.

They seemed fine to us, so we loaded 'um up in the trunk, leavin' the lid tied open a little to give them plenty of air. I pulled out on the highway. 'Bout the time I got'er up to thirty-five miles an hour, those dogs commenced to squawlin' and makin' all kinds of noise. We stopped and looked 'em over. I peeked in the crack we'd left in the trunk so they could breathe. They jus' looked back at us, real normal like. We coudden figure whut got into 'em, so we got back in the car and pulled out. Same thing happened agin… when we reached thirty-five, them dogs went nuts agin… I swear, we coudden figure whut was wrong with 'um. We pulled over to the side of the road and looked 'em over agin. They looked okay, mebbe a little wild-eyed through the lid openin' in the trunk.

Johnny said, "The trunk is big an' has plenty of room... Whut in the world is botherin' them?" So we took the dogs out an' he crawled in the trunk. He like to have fallen through a rusty place in the floor. Come to find out, under all the feed sacks, wuz a hole. One of them sacks had slipped through the hole an' got wrapped around tha' drive shaft. We figured that when we reached thirty-five the sack were jus' frammin' the fire outta tha floor—I 'spect it ner 'bout scared them dogs to death. We got some pond water an' made coffee. Then we plugged the hole with Johnny's tarp an' headed for home. That wuz the end of the frammin' and fussin' by tha dogs.

They turned out to be perty good deer dogs. They figured out whut we were after the first trip. We took an ol' deer dog with us and he taught 'em how to track deer. Didn't take 'um no time at all to switch over to deer huntin'. So for a few months we had us a fine set of deer dogs. But one evenin' we came home from a hunt while the circus wuz in town. As we drove by the park wher' they'd set up, we noticed a bear on a chain. He wuz gray around the muzzle, fat, toothless and older than dirt, but I reckon if you'd never seen one he'd be somethin' worth payin' a nickel to look at. It wuz staked out on the edge of the trailers and cages. I seys ta Johnny, "Wonder if tha dogs have forgot how to run ah bear... you reckon they'd take to that ol' thing?" He seys, "I don't hav any idea

128

they'd forget... why don't we let 'um have a look and see whut they do?" We pulled up about fifty yards frum where the ol' bear wuz staked out on his chain, got out and lifted the trunk lid a little more so the dogs could see.

All heck broke loose! Them dogs went plumb crazy an' busted the lid outta my hands and took to that ol' toothless bear. They circled him and nipped him in the butt—jus' like they used to do in North Carolina. The ol' bear wuz upset, cryin', "Ou-u-u-u-u-u... Ou-u-u-u-u-u..." while the dogs kept circlin' and nippin' him in the rear. Then things took a turn as ah big ol' elephant came after the dogs. Dust wuz flyin' dogs wuz yippin' an' runnin' around the moanin' bear an' the elephant near 'bout broke his chain tryin' to git to the dogs. You could hear people shoutin' and cussin'. People came runnin' with lanterns. (We guessed the elephant and the bear wer' buddies...) Anyways, we didn't hang around to find out whut would happen. We jumped in the car and pulled out for a palmetto patch down the road a-ways.

Things turned out okay though. In a little while the dogs got tired—or scared of the elephant—an' they trailed us up. They jumped in the trunk, hasslin' an' as happy as bear dogs could be. We didn't go by that end of town tha next few days while the circus wuz there. That wuz the first and last time we went on-ah bear huntin' trip.

CHAPTER SEVENTEEN

GROWIN' UP

Now I know you are still little gals and fellas, but I'm gonna tell y'all ah different kind of tale. I'm gonna tell you a tale with a moral. A moral is sumthin' worth keepin' for life—it's a life-rule. It's kinda like a compass so you'll always know whut direction yer goin'. Now listen reel close. I'll tell y'all at tha end how it fits for you, too.

There once wuz a little fella named Finis. He wuz just old enough to start cow huntin'—maybe he wuz about five years old at the time. Trouble wuz, he didn't know nuthin' about ridin' and workin' cattle. So the first thing he had to learn wuz how to ride a horse. His Paw started takin' him on the gatherin' trips. He'd wake up early, git his cloths on, pull on his boots an' grab his hat. He'd have a big ol' breakfast with the crew. Paw would take him to the horse barn wher' they'd saddle up the horses. His Paw give him ol' Brown to ride. She wuz gentle as a milk cow. Far as anyone knows, she never stepped on any of

131

the kids—even when they crawled under her to swat horseflies.

Now, Finis wuz too little to throw a saddle, so Paw set it for him. He'd lift Finis into the saddle, hand him the reins and a cow bell, which he tied to the saddle, an' off they'd go. The cow bell wuz fer Finis to ring when it come time to move cattle outta tha hammocks. (Ya see, he wuz so little he didn't have a strong voice an' couldn't whoop an' holler loud enough to move cattle. His Paw could also keep up with wher' he wuz ridin'.)

So the first thing Finis had to learn wuz how to climb in the saddle by hisself and he did figure it out. He'd walk ol' Brown over near a stump right outside tha' barn, get on it and climb inta tha saddle.

Next wuz how to ride and not run in tha' way of the other horses and riders. Now that sounds simple don't it? No, it ain't so simple fer a little fella or gal. Finis had to learn ta keep his balance in tha' saddle and how to hold on in a gallop; he had ta learn to rein tha' horse in the right way and to stop. All these things he had to pick up 'til he didn't have to think about whut he wuz doin'—it jus' had to become nat-ural-like and easy to 'im.

It took most of two summers and some cow hun-tin' trips throughout tha' year to make Finis a fair rider. He wuz learnin' real quick.

So Paw began to work on the next most impor-tant things for Finis: how to take care of his self, his horse and gear, an' how ta really be a help to tha crew.

He needed to learn whut he could do on horseback
and whut he ought not try. In other words, he needed
to know his limits and the horse's limits. Ther's sum
things ya don't do on horse back. Ya don't sail off
into a bog at a full gallop—you kin break yer neck
or back doin' such as that. Ya don't run a horse wide-
open in-ah pine thicket or in palmettos. An' ya better be careful when yer ridin' wher' yer horse might
step into a armadillo hole an' break a leg. You take
care of yer horse an' he'll take care of you. Ever time
Finis wuz gettin' ready to ride, he'd hav'ta check ol'
Brownie's legs and feet. He'd clean out her hooves so
she wouldn't git thrush an' sumtimes he'd have to trim
her feet when her hooves grew too long—so she'd
not split her hoof somewhers an' come up lame. Finis
had to learn to walk around her and be sure she wuz
lookin' fit. Wuz her eyes clear, wuz she lame or sore,
wuz her coat shiny and clean, an' did she eat good
that mornin? Things like that tell a rider if his horse is
ready to ride. He also had to comb out her mane and
brush 'er down ever' day and' to make sure his saddle
wuz oiled and in good shape. He had to be sure she
didn't git saddle sores, too. All the leathers on tha'
saddle an' bridle had to be in good repair, 'cause ya
never know when you'll need yer gear in good condition.... Ain't nuthin' worse'n havin' ta git off an'
fix sumthin' when it shudda been done at tha barn.
'Sides, the crew needs all tha help ready to work.

An' also he had to learn to work cows with ah
crew an' be dependable in his jobs. He'd only be ah

help when he could anticipate whut cattle would do an' whut the men had to do ta work 'em, called "cow sense." Cow sense is knowin' how to work cattle and whut the best way to work with them is. (Not ever'body has it—it comes natural to some, but sum have to work at it.) Paw worked it so Finis did ever'thin there wuz to do in cow huntin'. He started on the dip vat gate. Then he wuz movin cattle down the chutes. Once he had that down, Paw moved him to catchin' and workin' calves. Finis had to ketch the little fellas before he could handle the big stuff. (After all he wadn't any bigger'n ah earthworm with his guts slung out.... He'd need sum meat on his frame before he could tackle the big-uns.) Next, he started bringin' cattle down the alleyway—ta go git 'em out in the traps and crowd 'em in the pens. All in all, Finis wuz to learn ever'thin about cattle—gatherin', workin', vaccinatin', dippin, and sprayin' for flies, and returnin' to their pastures—includin' how to take 'um through gates, how to mammy-up calves with their mamas and keep a tally of the number of head.

So to this point, Finis had learned how to ride and not cause wrecks with tha other riders and horses; then he learned to take care of hisself, his horse, his gear. Ya mite say, he begin ta put it all together ... .

But there wuz one more thing he had to learn: Tha Big Picture.

He had to learn *why* they cow hunted in the first place. He needed some sense of how the whole thing fit together an' whut wuz mission, to learn to think ahead—not only when he wuz movin' cattle, but even years ahead. Things like would ther' be enough grass? Whut would he do if ther' wuz a bad wet season? Which pastures would be tha best to rotate cattle in? Most of all he had to learn grass and pasture management an' disease control.

When to worm and fluke tha cattle and when to vaccinate would have to be planned way ahead of time. He'd have to anticipate an' know whut the herds would need an' how their body condition would change durin' tha different seasons. Finis would have to develop tha skills to manage a cow crew—to tell 'em wher' to go an' who ought to be where to turn or bring 'um into the pens. He had to know market prices, the timin' of sales, which ones to keep and which to sell, how to negotiate with buyers an' tha' best ways to make a profit in tha' cattle bidness. In other words, Finis had to know the business an' whut it wuz all about—that's tha big picture.

Now yer probably askin' yerselves, "Whut is all this to me?" I told y'all that I'd tell you tha meanin'—so here goes.

You see, everybody has to learn three things in life: first, they have to learn how to get along in life. That's morals an' manners. It's how we handle ourselves—it's our character. The second one is how to work with others an' look out for them. It involves bein' responsible and reliable when workin' with other people. It's havin' social graces and getting' along with others. Some people call it "ethics". An' last, we have to see the big picture of life. We need ta understand tha mission an' tha plan that gives meanin' to life. That's understandin' tha big picture of why we're here on earth and whut our purpose is. This is the road to contentment.

Ya know, I've read of many a smart fella tellin' people about learnin' how to conduct themselves and how to get along with others. But I never read much frum these smart fellas about the big picture and the plan for people. They always seem to come short when it comes to that. Fact is they don't have a clue of our purpose on earth. They just don't get it—we're here for a purpose. My daddy said, "Always leave the land better'n when you got it. Leave a place for the wild life; learn to live with nature and not against it." His way wuz to always have two ways to pay back loans and be sure the other fella can make a nickel of two on trades. I guess the best thing I learned from him was that discoverin' our purpose on earth settles our lives into contentment. Seems to me that's the key to life.

Finis learned all these things well. He wuz a good man, he took care of his self an' others an' he understood whut his purpose on earth wuz. He had a life of contentment. He lived to a ripe old age. He had a good wife, sons and daughters and his grandchildren sat upon his knees. He had more friends than you could shake a stick at. There wuz standin' room only at his funeral. People still talk about him and remember him well. Boy, I miss him.

Somewhere in heaven, a vast herd of cattle are bein' moved to new deep-grass pastures. Ther's a man up front, wearin' a white hat, smokin' a big cigar— an' he's sittin' tall in tha' saddle. He directs the crew with his eyes an' hand signals. The catch dogs work without a word. Finis is home at last.

CHAPTER EIGHTEEN

THE NORTH CAROLINA DOGS

Once upon a time ther' wuz two fellas named Gus and Lee. They were the very best of friends. Wher' you saw one, the othern 'ud be not far away. They hunted, fished and worked together most all the time. One year they got this wild-tear of an idea they'd go bear huntin' in North Carolina. So they set up a hunt with a fella they heard about; his name wuz Homer Pace. So ever thing wuz set. Lee an' Gus loaded all their huntin' an' campin' gear in a cow trailer, hooked it to Gus's big truck an' pulled out for the mountains of Western North Carolina. The plans they made with the guide included all their groceries and a place to camp. Now "guide" might be a little stretch of the word for the "guide" wuz a mountain man.

They followed the directions to the mountain man's cabin. It wuz way back in the woods. Lee said, "Gus, I 'spect they have to pump sunshine back this far." Gus replied, "You got that right! It sure is a long ways to anything, ain't it?" When they finally pulled in the little cleared place near the cabin, it wuz late afternoon. There must have been fifteen or twenty dogs of all shapes, sizes, and ages runnin' around—it seemed so anyway. Ever one of them wuz barkin' and circlin' the truck and trailer. While they wuz markin' the tires, ol' man Pace stepped out with his shotgun in hand. He wore bib overalls, brogan boots, a flannel shirt and ah raggedy an' sorry ol' hat. He had a little astaphidity bag around his neck. His eyes were dark and you could tell he'd not be a man to mess with. He chewed tobacco and had a beard like Santa—but his wuz brown and gray instead of white. As he stepped off the little porch, the dogs circled him while waggin' their tails and grinnin' up at 'im. He looked Gus and Lee over a while before he said anything. Finally he said, "Who y'all lookin' for?" Gus said, "Mr. Pace? "Nobody calls me that—call me Homer" came the reply. He wasn't mad but very direct. Gus continued, "We're tha fellas frum Florida you said you'd take on a bear hunt." Homer's eyes brightened as he said, "Y'all come up and set. We'll put on some coffee." So Gus and Lee shook his hand and introduced themselves.

The coffee wuz strong enough to blister the hide on a mule, but it wuz hot and tasted of good well water. The whole time they talked, some of tha dogs wandered around in no hurry to really do anything, a couple of the puppies were play-fighting, others slipped off for a fat nap an' a few laid under Homer's chair or on tha porch.

The plan wuz for Gus and Lee to set up camp by a little creek runnin' down the mountain. There wuz a flat place there and the trailer could be on level. They set up cots, got out bed rolls, and hung a Coleman lantern up so they could see. In the morning, Homer said they'd head out to an area wher' the bears were, according to him, "thicker'n fleas on ah barn cat." (But he laughed when he said it.)

So early the next morning, Gus woke Lee; they saw the lantern light on in the cabin, so they called out to Homer. He yelled for them to come on in. He'd made coffee, fried bacon and eggs, made grits and had a fine batch of home-made biscuits hot out the wood stove. They bellied up to the table and had a good breakfast. Homer didn't seem to be in a hurry. He set back, listening to Lee and Gus describe the groves and cattle in Highlands County, Florida. He told about livin in the mountains, gatherin' herbs, gardenin' and such.

About 9:00 he got up, took his shotgun off the wall above the mantle and said, "If'n y'all want to see some bears, ya better come on!" So, the fellas hurried to the cow trailer, pulled out some fine, sleek rifles from the cases stored in the front of the trailer. As it turned out, ther' wasn't too much to bear huntin'… so it seemed to them. Ol' man Pace took them through the woods, through creeks and hollers, through mats of Mountain Laurels and Rhododendrons an' some places that seemed that even a bear wooden go. Gus gave out of wind in about forty-five minutes, but Lee lasted another fifteen before he come back and sat down by Gus. Homer came back grinnin' like a mule eating sawgrass. He sat down on a log close by, took off his hat and pulled a red bandana to wipe the sweat. He didn't say a thing. He jus' listened for the dogs. They must have sat there for thirty minutes when all of a sudden it sounded like every dog in the country had come together in a holler not too far off from where they sat. Homer said, "There he is. Mr. Bear done left his scent on his morning route." Off they ran after the dogs. It wuz butt over teakettle a time or two when Lee or Gus slipped on the wet moss in their cowboy boots. Homer never seemed to git in a hurry, but, boys and girls, he covered the ground. The dog sounds changed, becoming more intense and frantic—they'd caught up with Mr. Bear. There was all kinds of barkin' and dog sounds. "Woo-woo-woo", "Bark! Bark!", "Yap-yap-yap" could be heard coming through the woods. It was plumb pandemonium. Homer said, "Ain't that beautiful music?" referring to the dogs baying up the bear. Lee said, "If them d— dogs would shut up maybe we could hear it."

So they finally caught up with what looked to be all sixteen dogs circlin' a big ol' black bear. He'd growl and fuss. He swatted two of the dogs an' knocked 'um silly. He scratched three before they smartened up. The little fellas were content to stand out of reach an' yap at the bear. The ol' bear would try to run, but the dogs would nip him in the backside, causin' him to turn an' try to catch the one that nipped him. Ol' man Pace, Gus and Lee stood back a-ways and watched the fun. Homer commented,

"That's the bear that keeps comin' by my place ever year fer tha last ten years. He tore up the beehives over at my neighbor's house a year ago. Ephraim told me this ol' geezer caused him a lot of trouble last year. He told me to run him out of the country if I could." He didn't say much for a time. The dogs kept the ol' bear worried near plumb to death. But then Homer continued, "It don't seem right to me to kill him... he's jus doin' whut bears do to make a livin. I give Ephraim three of my finest dogs to keep the ol' thing away frum his hives—so far it's worked real good." He looked off in the woods with a far away look, like he wuz thinkin' some on some serious things. Maybe he wuz associatin' with Ol' Bear. Both of them were a little long in the tooth, getting' a little gray around the muzzle and both lived alone. Both of them didn't bother many people, though Mr. Homer had a nip or three of sour mash on occasion an' could get plumb saucy. Bear would tear up a bird feeder or a beehive, but that wuz rare—just about as rare as Homer Pace had his nip. In a way they wuz friends.

Gus looked over at sweatin' Lee; they caught each other's eye. With a nod only at Gus, meanin' he understood what Gus wuz thinking, Lee said, "Mr. Pace, if it's alright with we'd just as soon not shoot the ol' bear. We know you went to a lot of trouble gettin' us here, but it don't seem right to us." Homer brightened up at that word and smiled, showing his missin' front tooth. So he called the dogs off, let Bear ease off in the woods and they all went back to the cabin.

They had a big dinner about 2:30 that afternoon. Homer fixed smoked country ham, biscuits and gravy with grits and pinto beans. They all took a long nap that afternoon, all tired out and satisfied.

The next morning, Lee and Gus like to have never got out of their cots. They were so sore you couldn't touch them with a powder puff without them complainin' about the pain. When they did finally get up, Homer hollered, "Coffee's in tha pot … ." He had biscuits and cold ham ready for their breakfast. When Gus walked out on the porch with his coffee and ham-biscuit, Homer had three cane poles layin' on the porch. "Whut you getting' ready to do?" he asked. "Well, I figured since y'all wuz a little sore frum all the runnin' in the woods, we'd go trout fishin'. I know a good hole or two wher we can catch some gooduns. Mite be a little hard to git too 'um but it'll be good eatin'."

So off they went, each carryin' a long cane pole and some ol' handmade plugs, which were made to look like little fish an' had treble hooks on them. He carried them down a trail beside a fast, roaring creek with water tumbling over big rocks and boulders. The thrashing water wuz so loud you had to raise yer voice for someone to hear you speak. Mist covered the rocks, trees and the soft mats of dead wet leaves. Down and down, round and round they went for a good hour of winding and twisting mountain trails next to the stream. The air was cool and musty but pleasant. Sometimes it'd be so slick they'd have to be careful an' move slow to keep their footing. The cane poles were pure misery to get through places at times. But somehow they made it to a place where the waters spread out into little pools.

There, they took a breather and watched the quiet water. Over these pools, thick limbs hung like dark green drapes. The trickling water was clear and quietly moved in little eddies and whirls as it meandered down stream. If they sat real still, they could see the biggest trout you ever saw, layin' up in the dark cool places. Homer asked them to sit ther' while he showed them how he caught trout. He eased around the thick tree limbs, over and under some of them on his way close to the holes where the fish lay. When he got where he wanted, he'd took his long cane pole and tied one of the plug-baits on the short six-foot line. He'd ease the bait out over the water and whip it under the tree limbs—right in the area of the trout. On the third cast, the water boiled and exploded as a big trout hit the bait. He pulled him out and hollered, "Now, y'all try it!"

So Gus and Lee had a ball, each catching a big trout. They had three big trout in all. They weighed from about fifteen to twenty pounds (Course you know all fisherman lie…). On the way back to the cabin, when they stopped for a rest, Homer smiled, saying, "Ever' now 'n then sumbody will ask me, 'Homer, where'd you catch them fish?' I'll stick a finger in ma mouth and tell them, 'I hooked sum of them up here in the roof of their mouth, and sum over her' on the sides of their mouths... .' They'd figure out real quick I ain't tellin' them wher' I go for the big fellas."

They cleaned the trout, fried them, an' made slaw, green beans, hush puppies and cornbread. It was a regular feast. They sat on the porch after supper and talked 'til after sundown. During the talkin', all the dogs had settled down for the cool night. Every now and then one would slip off in the woods and listen, smellin' the air. All of a sudden, one dog opened up with the loudest howling you ever heard. Dogs come from under the cabin porch, boiled out of holes, off the porch and every where... all fifteen pulled out after the first one that opened. Homer quietly remarked, "It's probably a panther ... one comes by couple times a year. Get yer shoes on, we'll go see. Bring yer flashlights, too."

So off they went following the sounds of the dogs. It wasn't long at all when Homer, Lee and panting Gus caught with them. Up in the tree, on a limb that hung out over the trail a-ways, was the biggest darkest panther they'd ever seen. The lights shinin' in its eyes caused it to yowl a cry that would scare John Brown's mule to death. Lee said later, "It sounded like a wild women or one of them banshees you hear about." (Me myself, I wouldn't know what banshee sounds or looks like. I wonder if it's like a cootagator? I haven't seen one of them either.)

Anyway, the dogs wanted to run that cat more'n anything. Mr. Panther closely watched the activities below him, but he seemed nervous and mean, too. (Reminds me of an ol' gal I once knew...)

After a time, Panther made a run for it. The dogs was bouncin' over each other getting out of the way when the big cat came down the tree. A couple of the braver ones tried to pull the ol' nip-in-tha-butt trick they used on the bear but they paid dearly for the mistake. The panther was twice as fast as the bear and tore the ear on one and like to have pulled the hide off the shoulder of another. They smartened up real quick. The panther put it in high gear and pulled out for far away places—anywhere but where all the yappin' and barkin' was.

Lee and Gus laughed 'til they were silly about the pandemonium of sixteen dogs treeing a panther. They called the dogs and returned to the cabin. They all, dogs included, slept like tired babies that night.

Gus and Lee had to start packin' up to go home. Gus asked, "Whut you reckon those dogs would do on a deer hunt?" "I reckon they'll run any game that has a scent" said Lee. They looked at each other and smiled. Gus thought out loud, "Yeah, let's try to buy a couple of the good ones."

So the game began. In the one corner was two Florida Crackers teamed up against a North Carolina mountain man on a dog tradin'. It went something like this:

Gus: "What'd you take for that brindle and the Red Bone Hound crossbred?"

Homer: "Who ol' Buck and Jake? They ain't fer sale."

Lee: "Man, you got more dogs than the law allows—surely you can spare a couple."

Homer: "Naw, I need ever one of 'um."

Gus: "Why? You could pare down to ten and not miss a beat."

Lee: "Come on, Homer, what'll you take for them two and the black hound puppy… and the big white gyp?"

Homer: "Grits and Sally, too? I don't think so… them four are my best dogs. I need 'um to train any new ones I git."

Gus: "Now, Homer, you know you can part with some of these dogs. Tell you what, we'll give you $100 for half of them. That way we'll be sure to get a few good deer dogs out of that many."

Homer stuck his thumbs in his bib overall straps and looked out in the woods. Finally he said, "That's a heap of money… I might let four go for that but I'll pick two and you pick two. I'll pick whut I think will be good deer dogs. But Buck, Jake and Sally are not for sale."

Lee: "Look we ain't had so much fun as we have with this bunch of clowns. We need some deer dogs— why don't you sell us three you pick and Buck for $150?"

Homer: "Well, seein's how y'all are such good company an' all, I might take $200 for what you offer."

Gus: "Whut would you take for the whole bunch?"

Homer: "Shoot! As good a dogs as they are, I wouldn't take $500."

Lee winked at Gus and, figurin' they wuz just talkin', said, "Would you take $300 for the whole bunch?"

Homer: "That's a deal—$300 for the lot."

All three men grinned like possums eatin' watermelon.

So the next mornin' they packed all their gear in the truck and loaded sixteen dogs in the cow trailer. As they shook hands and said goodbyes, Homer said, "You Florida boys come back now, anytime..." as he was stuffin' the $300, cash money, down the front of his overalls.

But that ain't tha end of the story. Gus and Lee went back to Highlands County. They spent $500 on dog pens to hold the lot of them. They took the bunch down to the vet and had them vaccinated for all the things dogs needed. The vet wormed them all. It took almost an hour to treat the whole bunch. Lee said he couldn't remember all the names except Buck, Jake, Sally and a few others. So he let the vet start naming them. He named one Ring, others were Bob an' Pied. He was running out of ideas when he come up with, Judy, after his first wife (cause the dog bit him), Miz Beasley, cause she'd just left the clinic, Yeller, Clem, Whitey, Brownie, Blackie, Brindie, and Festus were some of the others. It really didn't make

much difference 'cause Gus and Lee called them
"Hey, Dog" most of the time. They laughed and had
a time catchin' each dog, which had to be caught in
wadded up knots of waggin' tongues an' tails and
sixty-four paws constantly movin'. Three of 'em loved
people so much, they kept tryin' to get back in line.
Every one of them was barking for all they was worth.
Lee held, "I don't think any of them have been to
town before."

After huntin' season, the vet saw Gus and Lee.
He asked them how the deer huntin' went this year.
Gus bust out laughin' as Lee said, "We unloaded the
bunch of them in the Everglades on fresh deer sign.
They pulled out like a house afire. Four of them
never came back. Two jumped in tha water to cool
off a little, right next to a gator... like to have scared
them to death—they wooden come out of the trailer
after that. We give them to one of Gus' men for pets
for his kids. Six of them went over to a camp about
a mile away. They stole 'em—left with 'um the next
mornin'..." Gus took up the tales, saying, "Two of
them never left us; they walked behind us so close that
when we stopped they'd bump into our legs. Scared?
I think! I named them 'Goodness' and 'Mercy' after
the Bible verse that sez, 'Surely Goodness and Mercy
will follow me all the days of my life....'" Lee inter-
jected, "I called 'em 'click-a-long hounds', cause my
heels kept bumpin' their bottom jaws an makin' their
teeth click as we walked."

Gus laughed and continued, "We gave one of them to a watermelon farmer at a gas station in Immokalee. One moved in next door to my house after he dug outta his pen. I didn't have the heart to take him away from that little girl she took up with."

Lee continued, "Out of the whole lot of them, we had three left. Gus got Jake and I got Buck. They're the best deer dogs we ever had. We got one female left—Ol' Judy and she still bites. We thought we'd go by an' tie her to yer ex-wife's Cadillac, seein's as how they are so similar in disposition an' all."

The vet said, "That sounds good ta me ... I'll give you tha rope. Y'all sure spent a sack full of money on them dogs."

"Yeah" replied Lee, "But where can you have that much fun for $1000?" Gus smiled, saying, "And, too, we got some good memories, like deer an' bear huntin', treeing a panther and trout fishin' ... ."

Lee said, "Yeah, an' when we was leavin' North Carolina, tha memory of Ol' Homer sayin', 'You Florida boys come back now, anytime' as he stuffed our $300 in his overalls.'"

CHAPTER NINETEEN

THE LITTLE HORSE AND THE BOY

Boy, here we go with one my granddaddy told me. I guess I'll do something different this time; I'll tell you two stories at the same time. One is about a famous horse, the other about a boy.

Granddaddy said way back in the twenty's, there was a colt born at Claiborne Farms in the heart of Kentucky. This wuz tha' time known as The Great Depression. Shoot! The only things that made money wuz the government and the insurance companies. Everybody else wuz flat out broke. There wadn't work an' money wuz scarce. People did their dead level best to make ends meet.

Now this colt wadn't a Cracker horse, but he could'a been 'cause he was so little. He was a son of Man of War, one of the greatest race horses that ever wuz. They said tha' colt wuz a little too small, he ate too much and just seemed lazy. Oh, he grew alright but never seemed to reach his potential. From what Granddaddy said I suspect he didn't receive good trainin'. Truth is, a lotta trainers don't understand horses or, at least, most of 'em didn't understand this colt. Seems he got off to a bad start. To make matters worse, the colt never seemed to pay attention. That's whut they call it when they're training a colt or filly that just don't get it. Now 'cause of him not paying attention to his trainers, they tried to figure out a use for him since they thought he wadn't gonna make a racehorse. So they used for him to train an' build confidence in other young horses. Now the way they did it wuz to hold the colt back from runnin' wide-open so other colts could learn to run and win. They called him "the ringer" (that's whut they call a horse used to train other horses to win).

Always bein' held back an' not bein' allowed to win does something to a little fella or a gal. An' that applies to ah racehorse or ah man. Tha' colt got down-right mean. He wuz rank towards people and everthin' around him. Frum what Granddaddy said, I 'spect he was abused a little by trainers that didn't understand him. They thought he needed discipline. Truth is, he needed special care. When they whipped him for sumthin', he'd just get ranker towards them; he dished it out as good as he got. It didn't look good for 'im. He ended up bein' entered in whut they call, "claimin' races." That's the bottom of the barrel so to speak. Ya see, in claimin' races, any owner entered in the race can buy tha' winner of the claimin' race for a fixed amount of money. This wuz tha' way to equalize the horses in a race. If you thought you were outclassed by another entry, you could buy the winner for a low price. Nobody would chance runnin' a high valued horse in a claims race. Runnin' in claims races sure wuz a sorry end for the son of Man of War.

Durin' tha' time tha' colt was havin' his difficulties, a young man moved to California and opened a bicycle shop. Business was not too prosperous until he started workin' on automobiles. Then, things took off. He became successful and wealthy. They said, "It got so he smelled like money. His name wuz Mr. Charles Howard. He became a man of means with a wife, a son, a ranch and a fine house. One day, he left for a business meeting. His son, a young lad, got tha' keys to the farm truck and left home for a nearby fishing hole. The boy never came home agin. He died in a bad accident. Life for the Howard's fell apart ending in divorce. Charles Howard wuz a broken, grieving, an' lonely man.

As time went on, he started attending horse races. He loved horses since he was raised around them as a boy. He met a fine woman, they fell in love an' got married. He had enough money an', with some encouragement, began to think about owning and racing a racehorse. He happened to meet a down and out man, like those commonly seen during the depression era. Tom Smith was a true horseman. He had no job, but Tom had "the gift" of understandin' whut was happenin' in a horse's head. Tom didn't say much but, when he did talk about somethin', he usually was right in his assessments of horses and people.

One foggy morning, 5:30 it was, he saw a little horse walking out for the morning breezin'. (That's whut they call exercisin' on the race track.) Somethin' just caught Tom's eye. He said that little horse just seemed to look at him with a "whut-are-you-lookin'-at?" look. He must have seen somethin' in this little horse because he talked Mr. Howard into buyin' him. Here they were with a little horse only 14 hands tall at the withers—this 56-inch "pony" was far from tha ideal racehorse, though he'da made one fine Cracker cow horse. Thoroughbreds were usually 16 hands or more at the withers (64 inches or more). Tom is said to have sensed the little horse had the attitude of a racer. He was a little wheezy when he wuz breathin' hard an' a little lame but Tom Smith didn't pay any attention to that—all he saw the colt's "heart"!

Tom matched a down-and-out jockey, Red Pollard, with tha mean, bitter colt. Red had been abandoned by his father and mother as a small boy. Red's father made a tough decision durin' tough times. Red's daddy an' mama figured tha boy would have to make it on his own—they just drove away and left him. Red Pollard was a carouser. A get-drunk-an-fight kind of fella. Beaten as often as he delivered beatin's, Red was a broken, embittered, mean sort. He was truly an angry young man. But Red had one outstanding quality: he never took out his bitterness on tha little horse. Red always listened to Tom Smith. The first time Red got close to the horse, the horse pawed 'im an' ripped the pocket off his shirt. That little horse was meaner'n a snake. Charles Howard had bought the little horse for $2000. Tom said something that was prophetic, "He's so beat up, it's hard to tell if he can do it right."

One of the first things Tom did was to take Red an' the horse away from the horse farm, out to the country. "Ride him as far as he can go," He told Red, "take him until he stops—just as far as he can go. Let him be a horse again."

Sumtimes, horses need a friend that stays with them all the time. You know, sumthin' to keep company with. Tom tried to get the little horse a "buddy" for the stall. The first thing Tom picked for a companion wuz a goat. It didn't last long—tha' horse kicked it outta tha' stall. But finally a hound dog and the horse bonded as buddies. Life wuz a little more tolerable for the little horse after he had a buddy. During the early training, Tom said that the little horse was "sleeping" on the track. They just couldn't see that he was interested. This was the case until one mornin's exercise session, the little horse came up behind a running horse which wuz also in training. On a curve on the far side of the track, Red said it was as if the little pony just looked tha running horse over and then shifted into a gear that was totally new. He said it was like an invisible boost of raw power. Tom said, "Sometimes, they just hanker for a little competition." That was the beginning of a racehorse career!

That little horse went on to stun the racing world with his pure running talent. Winning six consecutive races in a row, he was a lift to a depressed nation as he was the little horse that overcame all odds to win! The whole nation seemed to need a hero an' this horse wuz a hero. He lost one race, however. In that race, the winning horse came up on his right side and swept past him. When Red was asked why he had let it get away from him, he revealed that he was blind in his right eye. The injuries Red got in some of his barroom brawls had been the cause of the sight loss and the loss of that one horse race.

The little horse won race after race. Not only just win, he beat the Triple Crown winner, War Admiral, in a heads-up race. War Admiral was a monster of a horse—why he'da made two Cracker ponys. Tha' professionals said, "There's no logical way that tha' pony could beat War Admiral!" It made sense 'cause he really wuz ah awesome an' powerful beast. The race was set up on a bet with War Admiral having the advantages. The distance was longer than the little horse had ever run. He had to be trained to start from a standing-start rather than from a gate—as a part of the bet—with only two weeks training time before tha' scheduled race. But he won that race convincingly. Early in the race Red held 'im back for a time, lettin' the pony again size-up the competitor, and in typical fashion, that little horse kicked in tha' extra thrust needed to pass the big horse. He went on to race a spectacular series of races until he got a severe injury in his right front leg. Mr. Howard and Tom retired the little horse. It looked like the end of his career. But soon, to his surprise, Red discovered the little horse wuz runnin' hard in the pastures—he wuz healed! Red saddled 'im up an' soon discovered that he still had tha' racer's heart. The little horse returned to racing and won again! He had heart. Ya see? This broken horse, bought by a broken, lonely man, trained by a down-and-out trainer, and, ridden by an angry, half-blind jockey made racing history at a time when the whole nation needed ah up-lift. They had their hero in this little horse. Red once said, "Everyone says we fixed this broken horse but the truth is he fixed us—I guess we fixed each other."

Now, for the second story.

There was a man who was broken and bitter. He had been married twice. Both marriages had fizzled for different reasons. He never said much about it so I don't know tha' details an' I really don't care much about it anyways. But it's safe to say, he was truly a lonely man. Let's call him Jim. He often rode on his ranch in deep meditation. Some said that he didn't have much to say. Some said they thought he was angry. He would ride for hours, content to be by himself. That was the case until Jim saw this Kentucky woman in Miami, Florida. She was a divorcee who had moved to tha' big city, determined to make it alone. She had held as many as three jobs simultaneously to make ends meet. She was an abused, beaten woman who had low self-esteem. Divorce was quite a stigma in those days. She didn't trust any man, for

good reasons—the ones she'd known were untrust-
worthy or rotten.

Jim saw her weekly or so as he often had business in
tha' city. He was an agricultural loan appraiser. After
a few quiet coffee breaks, Jim introduced his son and
daughter-in-law and asked her out for dinner with his
family. She politely declined the first time or two but
finally, she agreed to go to dinner with them. That was
the beginning of a grand life for both of them.

Now tha' woman had a son who went to school
in Kentucky—he hated Miami and didn't want to
live there. He figured that if he was going to have to
fight, he wanted to be on his own familiar turf. Jim
and tha' boy's mama married in February 1960. They
asked the boy to come down to the ranch for a break
after graduation. Here was a whole new world of cattle, woods and wildlife, horses, Cracker folk an' cowboys and ah stable family. That boy was in heaven!
Not long after he arrived, he and Jim took long quiet
rides together. In sharp contrast to his previous hab-
its, Jim started to talk about history, people, places
and nature. He had long talks with his new wife. She
would often pour out all the pent-up venom of a life
started sour for hours sometimes. He listened and listened. Gradually, she healed. But the boy—he was a
piece of work! Jim told his new wife that if he could
have gotten the boy when he wuz eleven or twelve
years old, he could have saved him a world of grief.

One day, on one of those long quiet rides he and
the boy often took, Jim pulled under a massive oak.

He told the boy that it was time they had a little talk. Jim asked if the boy knew why he married his mother. The boy speculated that he thought they loved each other. Jim agreed. He asked if the boy knew that he knew his mother had told him all about her son. The boy was not sure what he had been told before they met as stepfather and stepson. He then quietly proceeded to tell the boy that he loved his mother and he said, "Because I love her and you are her son, I love you and take you for my son as well." He told the boy he could do anything he wanted there on the ranch but there was only one requirement: "Don't ever lie to me about anythin', no matter how much it hurts." That day a covenant was formed between a lonely man and an abused, forgotten, emotionally immature boy. Tha' boy became a son and went on, after a few stumbles, to become a man. Jim kept telling the mother, "Let him alone—let him try his legs—let him make some mistakes an' learn." It sounds very much like the man who said that the little horse needed to learn to be a horse again, only in this case, the boy needed to learn how to be a boy again. There were some tense times when the boy fell off his horse, got hooked by a cow or two, chose some poor company, but, all in all, the boy grew up. He went on to college an', like the little horse, sized-up tha' competition. He also had to come from behind in many areas of college. But he not only finished college, he did well. He married a good woman, a custom fit for him. Tha' boy-turned-man never forgot the first man who ever showed him he loved him as his own son under an oak tree. He never forgot the lessons the man taught him about God, people, history, nature, loving and being loved. He became an overcomer, too. All of it was mostly due to the unconditional love of the man named Jim, who could see tha' boy's "heart" an' knew whut wuz goin' on in his head.

So what is the point of these two stories? In the first, ther's a broken man, a broken trainer, a broken jockey and a broken horse. In the second, we see a broken man, ah bitter an' broken woman, a sour boy who needed more than anything to learn to be a boy and a man. The horse and the boy had one thing in common: they both came from behind in most every way.

Ya see, we should never give up on horses or people. All it takes is the right individual to see their "heart." Sometimes it takes winnin' some races. Sometimes, broken people an' horses need a little understanding as to what is going on inside their heads. We can learn from these stories. Sometimes, we need to learn to be human. Sometimes we need a little coaching, encouragement, and the freedom to fall an' git back up and go agin. But, above all, we need to know there's someone who loves us an' unconditionally supports us.

The little horse was named Sea Biscuit. He could well have been named "The Overcomer." He will be known forever for his heart. Oh, by the way, in the second story, I wuz the boy.

CHAPTER TWENTY

LOYALTY

Many years ago I was told a story that touched my heart. It's about a Cracker and his dogs. One might immediately think the dogs in this story were cow dogs or what we call "Florida Cur Dogs", referring to the old Florida cur dogs used for working cattle or hog hunting. But, no, the dogs in this story were not what you'd think.

As the story goes the man was a Florida cattle rancher from a pioneer family of settlers in the marshes and piney woods north of Lake Okeechobee. His cattle were the typical cattle of the times, being a combination of old Spanish cattle left behind when the Spanish abandoned Florida somewhere in the 1500's and the Brahman Breed.

Maybe I should take a rabbit trail and explain some things. Most people don't know that Floridians has been herding cattle for some 500 years, starting with the Spanish, then the Seminoles and lastly the settlers from Georgia, South Carolina and other places in the South. They commonly called these old generations of cattle "scrub cattle." In fact, some of the early properties of the pioneers contained wild herds of scrub cattle. Many of the first Florida settlers began to collect and manage these wild herds for sale to Cuba, Key West and during the War Between the States, to feed the combatant troops. When I say, "manage" I mean they "cow hunted." The cattle roamed free in the woods and marshes of old Florida. The Crackers simply adapted to the conditions, following or "huntin'" wild cattle, roping, marking and branding them as they caught them. It was a rough life full of all manner of danger. In the mid-1800's it was perilous times in early Florida; there were forays into the state by both sides during the war. The Yankee and Confederate troops bought or stole and gathered cattle for shipment during that terrible war.

Sale prices of scrub cattle herded to Punta Rassa, near Ft. Myers, and to Forts Tampa and Pierce ranged from $5 to $10 a head, depending on their body condition. The sale of these cattle brought trunks full of gold doubloons to the lucky and resourceful cattlemen who made the long cattle drives. Herds were stolen by rustlers or lost by natural disaster or simply were lost to wolves, panthers and bears.

Cowboys were shot from ambush and there were fights over grass during the early days. One town, Tater Hill, was notorious for the number of rustling outlaws that thrived there for a time. Kissimmee and Ft. Myers was also cow towns at the time. After a famous nasty gunfight, which cleaned out the outlaw gangs, Tater Hill was restored to law and order. It was later renamed Arcadia. This was a time when the Caloosahatchee River flowing westward from the vast Lake Okeechobee toward Punta Rassa was clear water. The sun reflected off the sandy bottom through the blackened waters.

The old Cracker cattlemen didn't at first seem to have need for gold; they lived off the land, utilizing wild game and little gardens for their sustenance. Gold from cattle sales was later utilized to buy land as more and more pastures were fenced by some settlers; gold was more important to Crackers then. Vast land purchases ensued and fences surrounded these early ranches. Even though fences became more common, cattle stealing remained a problem in areas. More often than you would think, shots rang out through the woods to warn thieves. There's nothing like the message sent by a bullet skinning the bark off a tree near your head.

The remnants of scrub cattle were small, tough, wild and the little "scrub bulls" were meaner than cornered snakes. There were small herds of wild scrub cattle on fenceless areas in Florida as late as the 1940's. Scrub cattle were so small and weighed so little that cowboys could catch and hold them for ear marking and branding to signify ownership. Community cow pens were common then. The cowboys in an area would cooperate during the gathering of free-roaming herds. They'd cow hunt in the woods, marshes and wild country, taking the collected cattle to near-by pens. Ear marks and brands on the cattle indicated the ownership of them. Each cattle-man had a specific ear marks and brands that proved ownership. There were multiple intricate combina-tions of ear marks and a variety of brands. These marks and brands were later registered and recorded with the state as proof of title. At these community pens they'd work the cattle, determining which calf belonged to which man's cow. This was called, "mam-myin' up." Once the pair was identified they'd work the calves with the man's marks and brand. They'd mark and brand, de-worm, castrate the male calves, give mineral supplements to the herds and turn them out to free-roam again.

In the center of the state in the Kissimmee River Valley, the cattle tended to roam to northern areas in the summers and south toward Lake Okeechobee in the winters. This natural roaming pattern was due to the overwhelming numbers of mosquitoes that hatched during the summer rainy seasons. In the early days before fencing, cattle would bed on the sand roads of what would someday be major high-ways. The tourists would come upon them lazily chewing their cuds in the middle of the roads in the night. They would toot the horns or one could hear the old "ah-hoogah" of the Model T Fords at these times. They'd also race the motors to encourage the cattle to move out of the way. Of course, as more and more land was fenced the numbers of roaming herds slowly declined and the cattle were more confined.

Confinement on fenced ranches made management more critical. Pastures had to be developed, grasses planted, land cleared and the excessive water drained from big wetland marshes. This was a time of rampant development when many canals were dug to control water.

The problems with the drainage and development would not surface for many years afterward. Hurricanes and high water influenced decisions of aggressive developers and willing politicians. Pristine waters became choked with debris and unnatural plants and became stagnant. The Seminoles were the first to understand the implications of the intrusions into natural Florida. Their warnings were not heeded as the white man brought land-ownership and development ideas to fruition. As a result, especially with land booms and the influx of new people, more drainage and clearing were considered necessary. Years later, the meandering Kissimmee River was converted to a ditch, allowing tons of contaminating organic matter and run-off into big Lake Okeechobee. Old timers warned that the changes would alter the natural flow and self-cleansing aspects of things, but their warning fell on deaf ears. Many years later the environmental effects of the altered Kissimmee came to light. It was "discovered" that the old timers were correct in their warnings.

In the late 1800's Florida pioneer ranchers began to apply the principles of "cross-breeding", known since ancient times. This method involved using

herd sires from greatly improved breeds of cattle, often called "purebreds." English breeds were
tried at first with some success but the East Indian
Brahman breeds soon showed their superiority for
crossbreeding in the hot and humid Florida region.
The use of "Brahma" bulls as sires with the old type
scrub cows resulted in an improved animal, called
"crossbreds." The offspring were bigger, stronger,
heat-tolerant, insect-resistant, and tough as nails in
the rugged Florida environment. They were not only
bigger and tougher they had some of the characteristics of the Brahman Breeds. For instance, they often
walked in little trails, one behind the other, in long
treks back and forth on the prairies, marshes and in
the rough areas called "scrubs"—just like the herds
of Wildebeest in Africa. They had a peculiar charac-
teristic of not being easily driven; but they could be
led by "leader" cows, steers or bulls, or even Cracker
cowboys riding white horses. Tales are told of big
light colored steers that were kept in herds simply for
their "leader" characteristics.

The crossbred Brahma herd seemed to have a ten-
dency toward what we called "babysitter cows." Many
of the mamas would leave their young baby calves in
groups in the care of a few cows that never left the
group. When threatened by varmints or cowboys on
horseback, the babysitters and separated cattle came
together in a group. Old timers said the groups would
form a protective ring around the calves with the
mama cows around them and the bulls would work

their way to the edges of the groups as a first line of defense. Another interesting trait of the Brahma crossbred was its tough attitude at being handled. Six-to seven-hundred pound scrub cattle were a thing of the past being replaced in several generations by a hearty nine-hundred to eleven-hundred pound cow. The Brahma bull and the crossbred cows were "hell on wheels" when prodded or aggravated. They would blow and come after anyone or anything in their way. They mainly wanted to be left alone, only becoming a terror when aroused. It was funny that if tamed when young they'd be as calm as yard dogs. But if left in a herd, the old instincts of wild cattle came to light. Crackers learned to use small tough Cracker horses, herding cow dogs and nosey whip-cracks to move them and keep them in a bunch.

Florida Cur dogs ("cow dogs") are somewhat unique. The old original dogs were mongrels of mixed origin; as they were selectively bred, many had some bull dog characteristics introduced to their blood-lines. The early Crackers soon discovered the advantages to having a dog that could help work cattle, hog, wolf, bear or deer hunt, and provides a measure of protection to them and their isolated homesteads. The Seminoles reportedly developed the early breed, paying little attention to anything other than natural cow sense—that instinctive trait to round-up, head-off and return cattle to the herd. Even before the Seminoles, the Spanish used what they called "war dogs" for conquering nations and probably for cattle herding. Herding instinct was a trait that was right down these dogs' alley. Big-chested, muscular but hardened from constant running, these dogs are said to have weighed upwards of eighty to ninety pounds. Nothing other than working or hunting ability was used to develop a multipurpose dog. During this natural selection process those dogs that developed skill and learned to work free-roaming cattle herds were cared for and bred to others with the same abilities; a useless dog was not worth a white man's nickel or was only fit for a meal in hard times. So it was not a breed as those developed in earlier years in other parts of the world. These dogs were specialized by breeding the "best" to the "best."

Some say handling these scrub cattle was a hard life but all agree that it was a satisfying one that far outweighed many other lifestyles. Anyone born to it was reluctant to change it—even as late as the story I now tell as told to me in the early sixties.

The man in the story was from the culture and heritage described above. He was a fine Cracker man—a born and bred Florida cattleman. He'd married a local gal and their family had grown over the years. By the time of the story, all the kids had left home, establishing their own families. He and "Mama" were content in their later years, satisfied with what they'd accomplished in a lifetime of work. The old man continued to tend his cattle, riding through them frequently to keep an eye on the calves and the herd. Conditions and weather had to be monitored in an effort to move cattle to better grasses or out of water-soaked pastures at times. He was used to long lonely Jeep rides, looking over the herd. It wasn't a chore; it was a pleasant life, filled with wonder and awe at the predictability of nature. Many seasons had passed over the years of his life. Drought and hurricane, ticks outbreaks and screw worms had come and gone. They'd survived and even thrived during these times. The kids always returned to the ranch to help him work the cattle in the early spring, summer and fall. They helped when he had any problems like downed fences, broken pen gates or with a cow having a difficult time delivering her calf.

Somewhere, somehow he heard about a German breed of dogs called, "Giant Schnauzers." Whether he'd seen one or read about them in a book, no one remembers. All we know is that he got a hankerin' to have one. He'd heard they were indeed large dogs, weighing about ninety pounds or more. They were reportedly quiet, fairly gentle with people and especially kids, big and strong, and noted for watchdog characteristics with loyalty to their masters as a strong attribute. Here again, the details of how he did it are unclear to me but he managed to locate a breeder of Giant Schnauzers in Germany. Through contact and negotiation, he bought two gangling puppies, having them shipped to Okeechobee.

They arrived in good condition and were so excited to get out of their big crates. They both ran in absolute joy upon being released from confinement.

Though a little stand-offish at first, they soon bonded to the man and became his constant companions. They indeed grew into dogs of a little over ninety-pounds. Big, muscular and rugged, these dogs went with the Jeep every time the man drove to check the cattle. They weren't cow dogs but they sure did enjoy his life and theirs, running otters, raccoons, turkeys and an occasional deer. But they always quickly returned to the Jeep (or into it) to be with the man whom they'd come to trust and love. They were noted for watching strangers when they approached the home or vehicle. It is told that they would even place themselves between a visitor and the man during conversations during these visits. They rarely barked, but rather gave a low, deep rumbling from deep in the chest when they sensed danger or wanted to warn of something they thought a threat. Somewhere deep inside these dogs was wolf blood.

Now I warn you, this is not necessarily a pleasant story but it does illustrate the title of it. On his last trip after a lifetime of them the man rode out in the pleasant sunshine on a routine afternoon round. The big dogs accompanied the Jeep, bouncing and play-snarling at each other in the sheer pleasure of the moments. They knew the routine: first, to the pastures; then, circle back through the woods to check all the cattle; then home. But today, this last day, it would not be a routine trip.

Twilight came and a blanket of darkness fell on the winter evening. A cold settled on the woods and pastures, flowing like unfriendly water on the land. The old man did not return home as expected. Mama was worried a little, but she knew he may be walking in because he got stuck or the old Jeep wouldn't start. It had happened before. She wasn't *that* worried since she knew he had the dogs for company and protection. "He'll be along anytime now," she thought. But as too much time had elapsed and her concern increased, in desperation, she called her son and a neighbor who called the Sheriff for help in locating the man. A team of volunteers and neighbors came to the ranch and began an earnest search. In the pitch blackness of the woods, men spread out, looking for signs where the Jeep had gone that afternoon.

Late in the cool night, through a low lying fog, someone spotted dim lights out in a pasture. He gave warning shots with his rifle and drew all the deputies and volunteers to him. They found the Jeep tracks in the dew-laden grass and approached the vehicle. Whether the motor was shut off or stalled out, they couldn't decide. The first man who arrived could dimly see the old man slumped motionless over the steering wheel of the Jeep. He was back-lit from dim dashboard lights and, apparently, the Jeep's battery was failing. The dogs began to circle the Jeep and prevented approach. With the arrival of several volunteers, someone screwed up his courage and moved closer toward the Jeep.

As I said before, "Somewhere deep inside dogs is wolf blood." The Giant Schnauzers reverted to the meanest and most viscous things than anyone could have anticipated. They took turns in defending their fallen comrade. One would get under the Jeep while the other would circle and attack anyone who approached. If approached too closely by more than one man they would both attack, literally willing to die for their master. Not knowing or understanding he was dead from an acute heart attack, the dogs only sensed he was defenseless and in need of protection.

This was a serious situation: no one could tell if the man was dead or in need of immediate medical attention. "We got to do something—we got to git him to a hospital if he's alive…" someone said. The decision was reluctantly made, "We'll have to kill the dogs to git to him."

There was quiet for a time while everyone considered the statement. You would think a bunch of grown cowboys wouldn't have hesitated, but they did; each knew it had to be done to potentially save the life of the longtime friend and neighbor. They had all kinds of thoughts flash through their minds. They all appreciated the expressions of dedication by these creatures. These men comprehended the depth of the bond between a cow man and his dogs—even if they were German dogs. The dogs must be forfeited to reach the man. So it had to be done and it was, quickly and efficiently.

After the old man was examined and found to be indeed dead, no one said much in the silence. In the cricket sounds and night calls of frogs, I guess each was thinking of what he'd just witnessed: an expression of true loyalty of two dogs for a man—that unspoken bond that develops in a man of the earth and his loyal helpers.

The old Crackers say of dogs and cow horses, "Most come an' go, but if a fella is real lucky, he'll have one good cur dog and one good cow horse in his life."

Some have more than one, but they're the exception to the rule.

CHAPTER TWENTY ONE

THE MEXICAN BULLS

I don't reckon I ever told about the time I went into Mexico lookin' for Brahma bulls, did I? Maybe you don't know what Brahmas are so's I'll tell you about them first. We always called them "brahmas" instead of the correct name of Brahmans. Us Crackers shorted it to, "bramm-ers." Way back when I was young we had a lot of cattle we called "scrub cattle" They had the look of the cattle abandoned or lost by the Spanish in Florida way back in the middle 1500's. The Seminoles took the strays also and were some of the first cattle herders in Florida. There were many of the old wild Spanish-type cattle roaming the woods and marshes way back in the forties and fifties. In those days, there were small, tough and mean bulls we called "Scrub Bulls", too. They were the sires of many calves, and served as the daddies of many generations. These cattle were small, in-bred, which means they mated within close families. As a result, they didn't amount to anything like modern cattle since they were stunted and small.

I heard old timers say that big scrub cattle weighed 600 to 700 pounds. Cracker cowboys could hand-catch and hold 'em for brandin' and ear-markin'. Their hair colors and patterns run from speckled to tan, brown, black and other combinations. Their ears were short and the horns were sharp and hard. They were able to slip off in the brush and you'd lose them if it wadn't for the cow dogs we took along. Them dogs could go ever'where the cattle went. Shoot! A fella with a couple good cow dogs could take a herd of scrub cows all the way to Punta Rassa or Ft. Pierce to ship to Cuba or up North. The old pioneer cattlemen didn't have much use for money 'cause they lived off the land. Tales are told of families that kept gold from the sale of their cattle an' hid it under their beds, but times changed and money became more important to them.

Around Okeechobee and Tater Hill there were no fences in those times. The wild scrub cattle roamed free on the marshes, scrubs and prairies.

It wadn't long before the Crackers realized that if they brought in good bulls, the calves would be better than the old scrub cattle. But there wuz a problem with that. They found the old English breeds like the Hereford and Angus didn't do good in the rough wilderness of Florida. They couldn't take the heat and high water, and the flies, ticks, worms and coarse grasses. There was talk of bringin' in some brahmas. They were tough and could tolerate the heat and flies and so forth.

As I said, Brahma's are really called Brahmans. They are an old breed of cattle. They ain't anythin' like the squatty or little cattle you see around and about on some of the farms you see when drivin' across the country. Once you see one, you'll never forget 'em. They come from India and there abouts. Why, some were used to pull carts in these old countries. Brahmas have a big hump on their backs at the shoulders, most have long horns and they're tall and have long danglin' ears an' loose skin under their necks we call the "dewlap." The big ears and loose skin allowed the brahmas to stay cooler than other cattle. They just seemed to be "built" for Florida.

If the Purebred Brahma bulls were put on the small native cows the calves would be better and would handle the heat and insects better. Sure enough, the brahma cattle were tougher and bigger than scrub cattle and more resistant to heat and insects. They could git around better, cover more range and did better on the native grasses.

My Paw made a point of telling me that Brahmas will not be driven, but can be led. We used to put a fella ridin' a white or gray horse out front of a herd so's they could lead the cattle. He also indicated that they were different in other handling characteristics, and to watch them close. Armed with sharp horns and ornery disposition, these tough cattle were a terror for the fella who wadn't paying attention.

So, the whole idea wuz to find us some Brahma bulls for our scrub cows. Better calves were bigger and plum hearty for our situation in the woods and prairies of old Florida.

But there wuz a problem at the time—ther' wadn't any Brahma bulls around Okeechobee. We asked around and heard there may be a few in South Texas and Mexico. So I decided to go over there an find us some Purebred Brahma bulls. Now here, the story gits interestin' ....

After I drove for days to Texas, I soon discovered that there wadn't any Brahma bulls for sale. In talkin' with several local cattlemen I heard there might be several in Mexico. They had been brought in from Brazil. I didn't have any idea of exactly where to start but the Texas cattlemen gave me some general ideas.

I drove my old Model T Ford down into the meanest country you ever saw. Ever'thin' there bit, stung, poisoned, stuck or poked a fella. The desert wuz full of scorpions, snakes, big ol' spiders, lizards and ever'where I looked I saw sand, dry gullies, cactus with nasty sharp thorns on 'em an' funny lookin' long-eared rabbits. And hot?! My goodness! It wuz so hot a toad would crawl into the shade of a cooking pot on ah camp fire to get relief.

To tell the truth, I wuz a little lost. Not exactly lost—I jus' didn't know where I wuz. I couldn't find the places the cattlemen told me about 'cause all the country looked the same to me. I wuz about ready to turn back when I drove around a little hill full of cactus and drove right up near a little Mexican man cookin' out in the boilin' sun on the upside-down fender of an old automobile. He wuz makin' his dinner. I stopped, got out of the Ford and walked over. He stood up an' smiled at me. I said, "Hidey" He jus' bobbed his head. I asked him if he lived close by. He smiled and bobbed his head again. I asked him if he knew wher' some brahma bulls were kept in this country. He smiled and bobbed his head. I asked him if his mama was still fat. He repeated the bobbin' head an smile. As I suspected, he didn't speak English. So I started over.

I held my hands up near my ears like the big ears of Brahma's and said, "Brahma bulls?" He lit up and got all excited, sayin, "Si, Senor..." I said, "Donde?" which I hoped meant "Where?" He pointed to the south and said somethin' in Spanish. I pointed to my Ford as I turned toward it and he got the idea that he would ride with me an' show me. We drove and bounced around for what seemed an hour... 'course, we couldn't drive fast or straight. In and around and up and down we drove as he pointed the ways to turn.

Lo' and behold, we drove right up to a small pen full of twelve mules. A small rickety wind-mill dribbled water into a tub that served as a water trough. The water ran over and down into the sand. I noticed one mule go over to the run-off an' put his foot in the mud. The muddy spot filled with water and the mule drank from it—instead of the trough. I guess he'd never had water from a water trough.

It wuz clear he thought I said, "Burros" instead of "Bulls." When I think about it, they do sound a little alike. Holdin' my hands up also looked like I wuz interested in burros or mules. A mule is the off-spring of a mare and a male burro. They ain't a burro and they ain't a horse. They're a lot like a horse but the ears are big and long. They don't look as refined as a horse, bein' a little mopey lookin'—kinda dull lookin' to most people. What would I do? I didn't need any mules.

I need to explain a little about horses, burros an' mules. They're different in more ways than their looks. A horse will be skittish and let you know real quick if they're gonna throw a fit, run or fight. When you approach a wild horse his instinct is to run. The fact is a horse's main defense is to run away from anything he thinks is a danger. You can tell almost instantly what a horse will do by the way he acts. He doesn't think like people an' horses ain't stupid... they jus' think different than people. A horse, once used to somethin' you do with him, will remember it all his life. When you try somethin' new to a horse, it takes about three times to teach him. 'Course, that works against people, too; they often make mistakes when trainin'. A horse can be trained to act ugly or right, dependin' on how he's handled. He'll remember a fella (or gal) for his whole lifetime if he has been mistreated or trained in a bad way. Many people really don't know how to train horses, but thank goodness there are some real smart trainers—ones that understand what is going on in a horse's head.

Burros, on tha other hand, in addition to being tough and little, seem to wait an' see what you are gonna do first. Burros seem to ponder people and situations before the commit to some action. They seem to study a fella when you approach them. Oh, they can run and get away but they don't seem to be in any hurry until they see your intentions.

Mules are a little of both in attitude. You can handle mules like horses but they can surprise you with an unexpected reaction. But to their favor, they're smart, tough, strong, reliable and often smooth to ride. A lot of people like mules because they're friendly an' get along well with people. They generally have enough sense to not over-eat foods that would make them sick or damage themselves. They work well to ride, back-pack, and can pull wagons, buck-boards and plows, too. I think if I had ta go a long distance I'd just as soon ride ah mule as ah horse.

So I thinks to myself: "Wonder if the man would sell these mules at a bargain price? They sure are in demand for farmin' durin' the times of WWII. I betcha I could sell ever' last one of them at auction in Georgia. Farmers need good strong mules for plantin' crops."

I said, "Quantos?" ("How Much?")

He said something in Spanish that went right over my head.

I said, "Five dollars?" and held up my fingers.

He grinned, saying, "Si, Si."

I said, "Mañana?" for "Tomorrow?" I knew that would work 'cause to him that most likely meant anytime the next day.

"Si, Si, Senor."

We load up in the Ford an' I take him back to his camp site. We said out confused good-byes and I drove back to the Texas-Mexico border into town. That night I called a friend of mine who ran an auction barn. I asked him what would be the market for twelve, healthy, young and strong mules. He said he could get top dollar in Georgia, "Probably upwards of $60 to $80, but you'll have to get 'em here."

So the next mornin' I talked with a fella that had a cattle truck and he agreed to take them to Georgia for a reasonable price. He was happy 'cause he had kinfolk there and he wanted to visit them. He was ready to go.

He followed me down into Mexico to the camp site; an' sure enough ther' wuz my little Mexican friend, all smiles and head bobbin'. I gave him $70— $10 more for the "tour" tha day before. He wuz tickled an' it didn't take Spanish to see that. That wuz probably more money than he'd ever seen in his life.

We loaded them in the back of the truck and pulled out for Georgia. We stopped along the way, rested the mules and fed and watered them. We reloaded and finished the haul by late tha next evenin'.

Ever' one of them sold for top dollar.

I wonder whut them Georgia Crackers thought when they got their new mule home... I bet that wuz a real sight to see: Mexican mules in front of a Georgia plow. I expect the mules didn't understand English either.

CHAPTER TWENTY TWO

PONCHO'S CAFÉ

I bet you cain't guess whut happened to me one time in Mexico. You're probably wonderin' why in the world a Florida Cracker like me wuz down in Mexico in the first place. I'll tell ya. I wuz there on a visit. A friend of mine used to go there ever' year on a huntin' trip. He wuz a big deer hunter and enjoyed the people and the country. He wuz a big insurance fella frum the big city up north. I never knew how he got hooked up with people in Mexico but he allowed he had friends in Texas—just over the border. So I figured I wadn't gettin' any younger and, too, he offered to pay for my huntin' expenses.

I drove into Houston, spent the night and pulled out for Mexico the next day. It wuz a long drive and some of the road were rougher'n a cob. I had never been to the desert areas of Mexico. But big deer lived in the area, just like they did in south Texas. I arrived in the late afternoon at a little sleepy town. The build-in's were a little grubby and run down. I met Mark at the hotel. It wadn't much until you got inside. It wuz clean an' comfortable lookin'. He told me we'd pull out in the morning. The huntin' lodge wuz about ten miles west of the town, but it'd be rough since the roads were only trails. We had dinner an' I went to bed early 'cause the next day would be a busy one.

It turned out that the next day wuz a bust. There wuz a blue line of clouds on the northwestern horizon that mornin'. Mark figured we wuz in for some rough weather. He called it a "blue norther." He said the temperature could drop 20-30 degrees in a matter of hours. "I ain't particularly interested in gittin' rained on and cold and that's whut's a-comin'." So we decided to sit it out for the day. That turned out to be the right thing to do 'cause the wind picked up, the mean lookin' clouds moved in over us and it began to spit rain. Sure 'nuff, it got colder'n a pickled pig's foot.

I spent tha day, readin', restin' and settin' around. As I wuz sittin' in the lobby readin' a Spanish newspaper (Truth is I couldn' read Spanish so it didn't take long to finish.), I overheard some people talkin'. They were speakin' in English. I walked over and introduced myself. They were two married couples from the States. Sounded like city folks to me but they were friendly. Said they wuz on a sight-seeing tour. Roger and Maryanne and Fred and Sally wuz their names. We talked about everything we'd seen. They asked me what a Florida Cracker wuz doin' in Mexico. I told them about the huntin' trip and Mark.

Roger said, "You all picked one fine day to go huntin."

190

"Yep, even though it's cold today, I believe it's a lot warmer here than in South Florida."

After talkin' awhile, I decided to take them to dinner. They were tickled about the invite to eat. They told me about Poncho's down the street a ways. Fred spoke up sayin', "We ate there two days ago and the food is good. They really put on a spread." Mark came to us and, after introductions, said that dinner at Poncho's sounded good to him. "Let's go," I said, "I'm buyin'.

Off we went, walkin' fast 'cause the wind wuz blowin' dust and rain down the street. To tell tha truth, Poncho's didn't look too nice from the outside but inside it was nice. There were some other Americans and well-dressed Mexican couples havin' dinner. Several waiters were movin' back and forth carryin' trays of food and pitchers of water and other drinks. A nice lookin' Mexican man figured us for tourists and spoke to us in English. He led us to a big table—big enough for ten or twelve people to sit.

The waiter, Ramon, said they had a good selection of foods and he would take care of all our needs. Come to find out, they didn't have a menu, they jus' started bring plates of food. Two or three waiters brought in avocados and mangos, fried dove and quail, roast beef and pork, tacos, enchiladas, tortillas and fried beans, rice and stuff I didn't recognize, though it looked an' tasted good. There was a big plate of desserts and a pie or two.

It made me uneasy. This wuz way more food than we could eat. I wonder if I had enough money for the six of us. On the sly, I pulled my wallet. I saw I only had thirty dollars and some change with me. The rest of my money wuz still locked in my suitcase at the hotel. This could be a real embarrassment an' a problem, too. About that time I see a fella come through the café from the back. He pointed at a table and a waiter hopped to, takin' water to it. The other waiters were movin', checkin' on the customers and watchin' the man.

Now I figured that must be Poncho. He wore leather breeches and vest with a white shirt. He had boots on and had silver spurs that jingled when he walked. He had dark hair combed back tighter'n a duck's wing and a three-day beard. His dark eyes missed nothin'. He meandered from table to table, greetin' guests in English and Spanish. People laughed and shook hands with him. He kissed the hands of the women. But he never failed to watch the whole room to be sure the waiters were doin' their jobs.

He came to our table and introduced himself. Yes, this wuz Poncho, an' he gave no last name. As we introduced ourselves around the tableful of foods, vegetables and fruits, when it came to me, I told him my name. Sally spoke up and said, "He's from Florida." At that, Poncho's eye flicked at me. He stared at me for an instant, smiled at all the guests at the table and moved on.

Now I was really sweatin'. This Poncho looked rougher'n a cactus. I wadn't so sure but the tales about him were true. They said he was an outlaw and come here to get away from someone or something. Believe me, he looked like an outlaw, too. I began to figure what I should do as the waiters kept fussin over us, bringin' us even more things to the table. They'd take the unfinished plates of food an' bring another of something just as good. I knew I didn't have enough money for this crowd and all the food. Whut would I do?

I figured I'd go up to Poncho and tell him my problem. I hoped he'd let me go back to the hotel, get some money and return without makin' a big to-do about it. As mean as Poncho looked, I really didn't look forward to the confrontation. He was sitting at a table near the front of the room, smokin' a cigar as I approached. He looked me up and down. He looked hard at my boots. One of my pant legs wuz hung in the top of my boot. He looked hard at me, stood up and said, "Yer frum Florida, huh? I figured as much when I seen you comin' up here." (His voice didn't sound like it had before—somehow he'd lost all trace of the Spanish accent.)

I said, "Sir, I got a problem with cash. I don't have enough money to pay for everybody's dinner. I wonder if you'd take this $30 and let me go to my room for the rest."

He broke into a wide grin, lookin' around to see if anyone was listenin'. He lowered his voice a bit and leaned toward me and said, "Shoot, Man! I'm a Georgia Cracker—don't worry about it. The bill ain't but $22! I buy the doves and quail for a nickel a piece an' the beef for nearly nuthin'. The hogs I raise myself off café scraps. The whole meal didn't cost me much. I have been down here for goin' on four years and makin' a sackful of money." He winked, "It don't hurt much to have a questionable reputation. I started it myself. These crazy tourists jus' love to be around a bad hombre like me. Boy, I sure am glad to see somebody from around home." He shook my hand. I sat down with him an' we talked about his home area of southern Georgia and my home in Okeechobee. We had a good visit.

Poncho said, "You ain't gonna let the cat out of the bag, are you?" I said, "No, Poncho; it's a real pleasure to eat with Georgia-Cracker-turned-Mexican-outlaw."

I returned to the table with my guests. I laid the $30 on the table and the waiters like to have broke their backs bowin' an' with all the "Gracias, Senor."

Later, Mark said, "What do you think about Poncho?" I said, "I believe it's safe to eat there."

CHAPTER TWENTY THREE

SLEEPY TOM

I heard tell of a horse that you might like to hear about. It wuz over a hundred years ago, in Ohio, that a fella named Stan Phillips first saw tha poor ol' thing. He wuz harnessed to a delivery wagon and he weren't ah perty horse neither. A sackful of people had owned this ol' rough and ragged looking creature. He didn't amount to much—as far as I know. Stan Phillips asked around about wher' he come from and things like that. Some people said later they noticed that Stan was out front of the store, talking to the ol' horse. He had rubbed him down, examined his feet and gave him a "horse trader's" look-over. Tha' current owner wuz plum dumbfounded when Mr. Phillips asked if the old horse was for sale. The horse's name wuz Sleepy Tom. "Why would you want that old, wore out wagon horse?" the owner asked. "Why, he ain't fit to do anythin' but haul freight or pull a beer wagon." Nevertheless, Mr. Phillips continued to ask if he wuz for sale. "Yep, he's for sale—but I still don't know why you want 'im."

Mr. Phillips went ahead an' bought the horse. Ever'one in tha' town thought he spent way too much time pettin', brushin', and talkin' to ol' Sleepy Tom. But Stan kept workin' with 'im an' he gained the ol' horse's confidence. After a time, he started runnin' ol' Tom in tha' local pacin' races at fairs, exhibitions an' such. Now pacin' ain't flat out runnin' like we do when we're cow huntin'. Pacers and trotter pull a little two-wheel cart with a jockey sittin' on it an' they never gallop wide open. They jus' get in ah rhythm at a fast trot or somethin' like that.

Stan would enter the races an' soon ever' body saw he had a peculiar way of racing—he would hold Ol' Tom back an' gather 'im up durin' tha' race. Whut do you think that means?

I'll tell ya'. He'd hold Ol' Tom back while all the other horses stirred around looking for ah openin' or ah clear track. By gathering, racehorse trainers mean Stan got him settled down an' payin' attention durin' the race. Ever' body thought Stan wuz plum silly 'cause he never put tha' horse out front durin' tha' race. At first, doin' this seemed to tha' crowds that Stan wuz creatin' problems for Ol' Tom.

Wellsir, that old broken-down horse began to win! They said it wuz puzzlin'. 'Cause durin' tha' races, Stan would hang back a little, letting tha' other horses spread out. They said they could hear Stan talking to Sleepy Tom durin' tha' race—kinda' reassurin' an' encouragin' him in tha' middle of the race. Stan wuz studyin' tha' situation, locatin' tha positions an' progress of the other racers. They said people could hear him calmly callin' Sleepy Tom for a little more power as he passed each horse. Stan would just sit in tha' buggy an' talk ta old Sleepy Tom through all tha' traffic toward the lead. You could hear him sayin' things like, "Easy, Tom; okay, Tom, let's go, Tom. Take it home, Tom." He passed horse after horse after horse an begin to win all tha' races they entered. Stan and Sleepy Tom raced all the local county fairs, keppa going on winnin' bigger races wher' tha' competition wuz stiff. He an' Tom won those races, too. In fact, Sleepy Tom began to win better'n anybody could imagine. He became tha' horse to beat in all those races. He broke track records an' even broke the pacing speed record by one second. That record still stands to this day! No horse has beaten Tom's record for over a hundred years.

Now tha' remarkable thing in this story is Sleepy Tom was stone cold blind! Stan Phillips had that uncanny horse sense an' the ability ta jus' "see" the potential in Sleepy Tom. He worked with 'im, wuz patient with 'im and gave the horse confidence in his quiet voice. Ol' Tom couldn't see but Stan could. He knew where to move, he could see the openings, he could see the race as it unfolded—all Tom had to do was follow tha' voice an' pay attention to tha' bits in his mouth an' tha' reins touchin' his flanks; he jus' trusted Stan, following his directions. Sleepy Tom may have been a beer wagon horse—ah horse only fit for pullin' a freight wagon—but he succeeded in becoming a world record holder in his lifetime of racing. Sleepy Tom holds that speed record to this very day. It is all based on trusting the one who knows what's ahead.

Now whut's this got to do with us? I'll tell ya… whut we often see as ah handicap or something unfair can be turned to a wonderful thing. If we're real fortunate we'll have people in our lives that are blessed with the ability to see what our potential is— even with what we think is ah handicap. Sometimes they tell us to trust them 'cause they can see where we can't. They have a feel for tha race while tha little ones may not. They see tha' competition better'n you can an' they know where ta put ya' to win.

That's why y'all's Mama an' Daddy always try their best ta' lead you tha' right way. Trust them to show you little ones the right way… They'll always put you wher' it's best in tha' long run. Ya see, life and livin' is kinda like a horse race. We all need somebody to help us run a good race. Why, we may not even know how to run the best race—but they do. So, like Ol' Tom listenin' to Mr. Phillips, listen to their soft voices when they tell you to hold up or to go ahead an' you'll do just fine. My Mama an' Daddy helped me. I helped yer Mama an' Daddy and they'll help you.

Well, it's gettin' late … time to put another log on the fire and go to sleep.

AUTHOR'S BIOGRAPHY

Howard Selby Jones was born in Henderson, Kentucky, and moved to south Florida during his teen years. He was introduced to the Cracker culture on the Williamson Ranch in Okeechobee, Florida. After two years at the University of Florida, he was accepted at Auburn University School of Veterinary Medicine where he gained his Doctorate of Veterinary Medicine. Following a stint in the Veterinary Corps in the United States Air Force and five years in a large/small animal partnership in Sebring, Florida, his teacher's heart brought him back to Auburn where he completed a two-year Dairy Medicine and Surgery Residency while earning his PhD in Ruminant Nutrition in the Department of Animals Sciences. After one year as the Dairy Extension Specialist for the Alabama Cooperative Extension Service, he returned to Sebring and purchased his former practice. And for twenty more years, he covered over a fifty mile practice radius surrounding Okeebhobee and Highlands Counties in the heart of his beloved Cracker cattle country. Now retired, Dr. Jones lives in the Blue Ridge Mountains of Western North Carolina with Hunter, his wife of forty-three years.

Made in the USA
Columbia, SC
26 August 2018